Ogilvie's Royal Command

Queen Victoria's granddaughter has married into the Russian royal family, and needs an escort to take her from Moscow to Nepal by way of India. Ogilvie cannot refuse a request from the Queen ... but these are dangerous times in India. Can Ogilvie protect his royal charge and still manage to keep his sights on a possible uprising on the horizon?

OGILVIE'S ROYAL COMMAND

Philip McCutchan

Severn House Large Print
London & New York

This first large print edition published in Great Britain 2002 by
SEVERN HOUSE LARGE PRINT BOOKS LTD of
9-15, High Street, Sutton, Surrey, SM1 1DF.
This title's first world regular print edition published 2000 by
Severn House Publishers, London and New York.
This first large print edition published in the USA 2002 by
SEVERN HOUSE PUBLISHERS INC., of
595 Madison Avenue, New York, NY 10022

British Library Cataloguing in Publication Data

McCutchan, Philip, 1920 -
   Ogilvie's royal command. - Large print ed.
  1. Great Britain. Army - History - 19th century
  2. Ogilvie, James (Fictitious Character) - Fiction
  3. India - History - 19th Century - Fiction
  4. Historical fiction
  5. Large type books
  I. Title
  II. MacNeil, Duncan, 1920 -. By command of the Viceroy
823.9'14 [F]

ISBN 0-7278-7129-3

Printed and bound in Great Britain by
MPG Books Ltd, Bodmin, Cornwall.

Chapter 1

It was as yet a little before the rains: the Earl of Elgin had not yet left Government House in Calcutta for the fresh cool of Viceregal Lodge in the Simla hills. Thus, on this mid-May morning, the Commander-in-Chief, sweating mightily into his scarlet tunic beneath the nod of white plumes drooping over the full-dress cockedhat, was driven through appalling heat to wait upon His Excellency. Behind the carriage horses, behind the turbaned figure holding the reins, General Sir George White raised a gloved hand continually, returning salutes, acknowledging the obeisances of Indians who bowed low as the British Commander-in-Chief went by, a great and powerful sahib who must not be offended by stares from unworthy native eyes. As the carriage neared Government House, bowling along a broad tree-lined mall that led to the currently deserted maidan, native India fell away behind. Here, although the great gardens contained thick tree-screens of palm and bamboo and beds of oleanders and euphorbias and Cape jessamine besides English roses, the architecture was wholly English, a virtual facsimile of an English country mansion on the grand scale, its grounds dotted with guns captured in battle by the British and Indian soldiers of the Queen. But as his carriage took him across the maidan and, changing its direction, into the grounds beneath the lion-crowned arched gateway at the east front, Sir George White had on his mind matters of more immediacy than the contemplation of the trophies of earlier wars. As Commander-in-Chief in India, first soldier of the British Raj, military representative of Her Majesty Queen Victoria, Sir George carried an immense and to a lesser man a daunting responsibility for the well-being and security of the sub-continent and its myriad human lives. And now, over the splendour of Viceregal Calcutta, over the peace and keen air of the Simla hills, over the always embattled North-West Frontier bordering the vastnesses of Afghanistan and the high peaks of the Hindu Kush, there hung a query out of St Petersburg, where the Czar of All the Russias, related by marriage to Her Majesty at Windsor, had issued a statement considered provocative enough for the Viceroy to be considerably put out.

The Commander-in-Chief's carriage, having swept past the gate guard's simultaneous click of presented rifle magazines and the crash and thunder of the General Salute from an infantry band, was driven around the east front to the ceremonial sweep of steps to the north, steps that gave admittance to what was termed the Breakfast Room and which in fact was a gallery of upwards of one hundred feet in length. Drawn up to one side of these steps was the Viceregal Bodyguard in their scarlet-and-gold jackets, shining boots reaching to the thigh, and striped puggarees, tall men and warlike. Again there was a resplendent band: again the General Salute thundered out sonorously, the first few bars of "Garb of Old Gaul". At the foot of the steps stood the Viceroy, ninth Earl of Elgin and Kincardine, uniformed and splendid.

Smartly, Sir George saluted.

'Good morning, General,' Elgin said, smiling.

'Good morning, Your Excellency.'

The climbing sun was a hard sphere of

metallic brilliance lofting over Old Court House Street beyond the grounds, and, more distantly, fashionable Chowringhi. Elgin came forward and took the Commander-in-Chief's arm in a friendly gesture. 'The others are here,' he said. 'We'll join them without delay.' With White, eschewing the stately flight of steps that were used only for visiting native and overseas princes and for the state arrival and departures of Viceroys themselves, Elgin made for a dark tunnel leading beneath the steps, a *porte-cochère* giving entry to a tomb-like space beneath the great Marble Hall of the ground floor: an incongruous entry after the sunlit splendour and the ceremonial outside, but one to which White had long since become accustomed. Unusually the Viceroy, attended by native bearers, men dressed, like the Bodyguard, in scarlet and gold, ushered his guest towards the office of Colonel Durand, the Military Secretary. Outside the room a havildar-major of the Bengal Light Infantry called an order to two sentries, who presented arms. As the native bearers vanished into the dim recesses of the basement area, the havildar-major opened the office door and stood back saluting.

Inside five officers rose to their feet: the

Military Secretary and the General Officers Commanding, Northern and Southern Armies – Lieutenant-General Sir Iain Ogilvie from the Northern Command at Murree, and Major-General Williams from Ootacamund in the Madras Presidency – with their Chiefs of Staff.

'Sit down, if you please, gentlemen,' Elgin said. 'We'll waste no time – I have a levée shortly, as you know, Sir George.' He nodded briefly at the Military Secretary, who walked across his office towards a large map hanging from the wall. Picking up a pointer, the Military Secretary laid its end upon the Khyber Pass linking the district of Peshawar with the remote, mysterious land of Afghanistan to the west.

'If I may have your attention, gentlemen,' Colonel Durand said in a crisp voice. 'I think you are aware of the facts, but there's no harm in my putting them in the proverbial nutshell, I imagine?' He lifted an eyebrow, received nods in response, and went on, 'Then here goes: the Czar has made it known officially that he intends to send an emissary to the Kingdom of Nepal – to Katmandu, in fact. We–'

White interrupted, 'Do we know yet who this emissary's to be, Colonel?'

9

'Yes, sir. The information came to hand only an hour ago.' The Military Secretary paused, giving weight to his next words. 'The Czar intends sending – a lady.'

White stared. 'A lady, by jove! The devil he does!' He turned to the Viceroy, showing amazement and consternation: about to speak, he was silenced by the grave look on Elgin's face. Checking what he had intended to say, he asked, 'Have we the lady's name, Your Excellency?'

Elgin's answer was startling enough. 'We have. It is the Grand Duchess Sergius.'

'Sergius! Elizabeth Fedronovna ... Princess Alice's daughter – by God!'

'Granddaughter of Her Majesty. This means trouble, Sir George.' Elgin, who had remained standing, walked across to the map and stood staring at it, hands clasped behind his back. 'The Grand Duchess will reach Fort Jamrud at the eastern end of the Khyber in three weeks from now, coming on from Kabul where she's currently resting with her escort, a regiment of Cossacks from the Astrakhan *voistro–*'

'But Your Excellency – the diplomatic considerations–'

'I've been constantly in touch with the India Office in London, as you're aware, Sir

George. To date I've been given no instructions. There is indecision, to use no unkinder word, in the air. It appears the Foreign Office has arrived at no conclusions yet. In the meantime, it is up to us to prepare, gentlemen.'

'For what, sir?' This was Sir Iain Ogilvie, crisply probing. 'What are the Czar's intentions – do we know this?'

Elgin gave a bleak smile, a mere grimace of twisted lips. 'Officially he has indicated a goodwill visit.'

'To Nepal, sir? Does the Czar imagine we have forgotten the Yanoff incident? Will you not yourself bear in mind the bloody campaign that followed in the Kanjut, against the Hunza-Nagir tribes? What *goodwill* has Czar Nicholas in mind, with regard to Nepal?'

The Viceroy shrugged; true, it had been a painful business when the Russian Colonel Yanoff, in crossing the Hindu Kush with a Cossack force to reconnoitre the Kashmir border, had violated the 1873 boundaries as agreed between Britain and Russia. 'Yanoff was in '91, Sir Iain, and is fast becoming history–'

'History my–'

'General, to receive indications is not

invariably to believe them. I propose to regard this visit as potentially hostile, I assure you!'

'I'm glad to hear that, sir. If the decision were mine, I'd damn well forbid it!' Sir Iain snorted. 'To cross British territory, even the Czar of All the Russias needs permission!'

'Undoubtedly – and it may be that I shall be given such instructions. The fact remains that to date I have not been so ordered, and the demands of a reasonable diplomacy must be borne well in mind, Sir Iain.' Elgin met the eye of the Commander-in-Chief. 'Yes, Sir George?'

'Sir, the Grand Duchess. Never mind her married state! She's an English gentle-woman, of Her Majesty's own blood. I think we can never accept that she would act against British interests!'

'Yes, General, you have put your finger on it. I agree with you–'

'Duress,' Sir Iain Ogilvie broke in flatly, 'cannot be dismissed, Your Excellency. We all know what the Russians are like.'

'Really?'

'A pack of damn foreigners with sadism as their stock-in-trade!'

'Patriots–'

'Patriots my backside, sir!' Sir Iain's face

flushed with anger, his Scots blood fully up. 'Sir, we are *all* patriots, but we don't behave like Russians in the name of patriotism! The damn country's run on slavery and – and blood!' Simmering down the Commander of the Northern Army brought out a large linen handkerchief with which he wiped sweat from his face. 'I say all this with the greatest respect, Your Excellency, but say it I do. That poor woman's not to be trusted and my view is, the visit should be forbidden and the party not allowed to pass Fort Jamrud.'

Elgin said mildly, 'Your remarks are noted, Sir Iain, and I'm obliged. But in the meantime we must prepare against such orders as may come from Whitehall. The first and most obvious consideration is the provision of an escort – and I would suggest it be at brigade strength. How say you, Sir George?'

White, lifting an eyebrow at his subordinate commanders, shrugged and said quietly, 'Your Excellency knows how stretched we are. Leave–'

'Leave can and will be cancelled as necessary.'

'Staff courses–'

'Can be cut short, General.'

'And sickness, sir.'

13

'Let the medicos busy themselves. A brigade's a brigade, I realise that – but we have two armies at our disposal, General! I would appreciate your constructive thoughts on the subject – quickly, if you please!'

White bowed his head meekly. After a pause he said, 'No doubt we can interrupt the relief programme. There are regiments on the high seas, being trooped to Bombay ... I can hold the time-expired battalions until next season if necessary and put up with the tooth-sucking. I think I can promise a brigade, Your Excellency, and I'd suggest it be detached from Murree rather than from Ootacamund–'

'Why, sir?' This was Sir Iain Ogilvie, forthright and belligerent. 'I'm a damn sight more stretched than General Williams is–'

'Yes, my dear fellow, I appreciate the problems of the Frontier, but time seems to be short and your soldiers are accustomed to the terrain, to hill skirmishes. I can replace, make up numbers from Ootacamund – that'll provide valuable training and experience for your fellows, Williams.' Sir George White looked up at Lord Elgin. 'A brigade will be provided, Your Excellency. May we leave it to General Ogilvie to make his own internal arrangements, and report the composition of the Brigade as soon as possible?'

Elgin nodded. 'Thank you, Sir George – thank you all, gentlemen. If we're lucky, the occasion will not arise at all.' He pulled a gold hunter from a pocket. 'My levée waits – pray excuse me now.' He walked to the door, all the officers rising with a rattle of swords and spurs. The Military Secretary preceded his master to the door, opening it and calling for the havildar-major on duty outside. As the door swung open, an A.D.C. was seen approaching at the rush. The A.D.C., a captain, halted and saluted the Viceroy.

'A cable from London, Your Excellency, marked Most Immediate.'

Elgin held out his hand and took the proffered cable form. Quickly he scanned it, then turned to the military commanders. 'My orders, gentlemen. It seems Whitehall has been separately informed by St Petersburg of the emissary's identity, and the Queen herself has been consulted – naturally.' He paused, his face showing strain. 'The visit is to be permitted and we are to provide an escort from Fort Jamrud to Katmandu. Political Officers are to accompany the escort, Sir Iain ... and to make their observations whilst inside Nepal.'

'Observations, sir?'

Elgin frowned. 'Is the meaning not clear to you? Are you forcing me to be precise?'

Sir Iain's lower lip jutted. 'I think it is necessary, sir. Must I take it that these Political Officers will fly not under their own colours but under those of the infantry and cavalry?'

His face stony, Elgin said, 'Yes, Sir Iain, that is so.'

'I see. And Her Majesty?'

'Her Majesty, Sir Iain?'

'Her Majesty the Queen-Empress, sir! Has she indicated her personal feelings and wishes?'

Elgin nodded. 'She has. She would feel it improper to use family influence and cause any awkwardness for her granddaughter, whose station is now that of wife to a Russian nobleman.'

'I see,' Ogilvie said again, his face still truculent.

'You have further comment to offer, Sir Iain?'

'None, sir, thank you.'

Elgin gave an acid smile. 'Then good-day to you all, gentlemen. Sir Iain, I shall expect your report of readiness as soon as possible after you have made your dispositions.'

'You shall have it, sir.'

'And remember who will be in your care.'

Ogilvie made no answer to that; but after the Viceroy had left the Military Secretary's office, he raised both arms in the air and shook them in the face of his Commander-in-Chief. His face almost purple, he roared, 'Damn it all, sir, what are we coming to? What has happened to the Army?'

White said with huffy impatience, 'Really, Ogilvie, I don't understand you–'

'You do not, sir? Then I shall tell you this: the Army and the country – they're being run by ... by an unholy alliance of damn spies and – and *grannies*!' Having thus spoken, Sir Iain stumped angrily from the room, his kilt swirling around thick thighs darkened with Highland hair – for notwithstanding Queen's Regulations for the Army concerning the dress of General Officers, he still wore the kilt of the Royal Strathspey. He left behind him the shocked faces and arched eyebrows of elderly gentlemen who had heard virtual blasphemy uttered by one of their own kind. It was inconceivable that Her Majesty should ever be referred to as a granny.

Chapter 2

On the parade-ground of the cantonment in Peshawar, right across the northern extremity of the sub-continent from Calcutta, the 114th Highlanders, The Queen's Own Royal Strathspeys, marched and counter-marched behind the battalion's pipes and drums in the harsh sunlight of comparatively – by Western standards – early morning. This was the time before the full heat of the day had struck; and there was a coolish breeze coming down from the north, from the snows of the high Pamirs. Sandy dust hung in the air around the marching feet. The warlike beat of the drums, the wail of the pipes, echoed off the barrack buildings and beneath the weight of rifles and shining bayonets men thought of beer in the canteen and of air stirred by no more than the patient movements of the *punka-wallahs* outside. There was a crowd ringing the parade-ground to watch the display of

18

regimental pride: officers of the garrison with their ladies, some of them visiting from Nowshera, which city shared with Peshawar the honour of containing the First Division of the Northern Army Command; a sprinkling of off-duty soldiers from other regiments and corps with their wives; daughters gaily dressed and carrying parasols, their attention, and that of their mothers, on the unmarried officers marching with drawn claymores ahead of their companies. Captain James Ogilvie, commanding B Company, was the target of many. Not only had James Ogilvie a fine presence and a first-class fighting record: as the only son of the Northern Army Commander he would be an excellent catch for any doting mother, and would one day inherit many square miles of Scotland, a castle, and a baronetcy. James Ogilvie, however, as his feet automatically kept the marching step, as his ears took in the drumbeats and the strains of "The High Road to Gairloch", as his right hand held steady the weight of the gleaming claymore's blade, was not thinking of women and of dalliance in the drawing-rooms of the cantonment bungalows, or on shady verandahs at the great balls that were part and parcel of Indian garrison life between patrols along the wild lands of the Frontier. His thoughts were rather of Bloody Francis Fettleworth, Commander of the First Division: Bloody Francis had personally ordered this parade; and Bloody Francis, who loved pomp and ceremonial, considered shows of strength and discipline to be very potent factors in the perennial Frontier business of keeping the tribes in check. In other words, the Divisional Commander invariably signposted his warlike intentions by ordering a full-scale parade. In addition to this, the grapevine had of late carried word, vague enough to be sure, that the brittle peace of the Frontier was to be broken by something potentially more serious than the customary patrol activity.

As the ceremonial drew to its close and James Ogilvie led B Company off parade, passing the dais where Bloody Francis was taking the salute, he noted, during his eyes-left, that a runner had approached the Chief of Staff who was showing every sign of an urgent wish to communicate with his master.

'Captain Ogilvie, if you please.'

Ogilvie looked up from the depths of a comfortable leather arm-chair. The anteroom was smoke-filled and peaceful, attended by self-effacing native servants: the sight and sound of the Adjutant was not welcome. 'Yes, what is it, Andrew?'

A shadow passed across the face of Captain Andrew Black: Ogilvie, possibly by impertinent design, had made the wrong response. In the 114th Highlanders, officers normally addressed one another by Christian name when not on duty, the one exception being the Colonel. But in Black's book the formal address required the formal answer. He scowled, moved restlessly, swinging his kilt around bony knees. 'A matter of duty, Captain Ogilvie.'

'Ah! Then sit down, Captain Black, and while you tell me about it I'll buy you a *burra-peg*.' Ogilvie grinned, indicating his own glass.

'Thank you, no,' Black said stiffly. 'Kindly report to my office. Do you not understand what *duty* means?' He swung away, his long, sallow face tight and angry. Ogilvie shrugged, caught the eye of Robin Stuart, a fellow company commander, across the anteroom, and winked. Black was too prickly for the Royal Strathspeys: he had never been one for the camaraderies of the Mess, holding himself aloof and stiff-necked. Obeying

21

orders, Ogilvie rose and left the anteroom. Outside he buckled on his Sam Browne belt over his khaki-drill jacket and took up his glengarry, settling it neatly in place on his head. Marching across the parade towards the Adjutant's office behind Black, whose long, rapidly-moving legs had already taken him halfway across, Ogilvie stopped for a word with Mr Cunningham, Regimental Sergeant-Major, who gave him a swinging salute accompanied by a crash of boot-leather as he halted.

'I think we were a credit to you this morning, Sar'nt-Major?'

'Sir! You were that, Captain Ogilvie, every man.'

Ogilvie grinned. 'A loud voice pays off!'

'And hard work, sir.'

'Yes, I know.'

'And first-class drill-sergeants too.'

'I know that as well.' Ogilvie paused. 'We may need all our precision soon, Sar'nt-Major. You'll have heard the bush telegraph, no doubt?'

'Aye, sir, I have. There's talk of someone coming through from Kabul. Of course, I'd not be knowing who it might be, sir.'

'Nor me either. It's all no more than rumour – but I have a feeling there's something behind it, and that it's about to show itself.'

'The men'll not be sorry, sir.'

Ogilvie lifted an eyebrow. 'Not sorry to leave the beer and skittles?'

'They appreciate that more after a spot o' fighting, sir.' Cunningham blew through his heavy moustache, rising and falling on the balls of his feet like a policeman, his pace-stick rigid beneath his arm. 'Besides, constant drill and parades ... they can become wearisome, sir.'

'True.' Ogilvie glanced towards the vanishing back of the Adjutant and nodded his dismissal. The R.S.M. gave another mighty salute, turned about, and marched away, left-right, left-right, pace-stick rigid still, free arm swinging from the shoulder, massive back straight, the tartan of the Royal Strathspey swinging, every inch a fighting soldier. Not much longer to go with the colours – and Ogilvie hoped he would live through the rest of his service to return to Invermore: life was cheap on the North-West Frontier and once away from cantonments, out in the wild hills, each man was a target for the hidden jezails, the long-barrelled rifles of the Afghans and the tribes inside the Frontier itself. In their years of

Indian service the 114th had lost their share, and more than their share, of good soldiers ... Ogilvie marched away, thinking now of the future: he had the feeling again, the feeling of imminence. Andrew Black had something special to impart, he felt sure: though why it should not be an occasion for all company commanders he did not yet know.

He was not left in doubt: Black, in his office, came quickly to the point.

'You will have heard rumours, as I have done, Captain Ogilvie. They have substance.'

'And the substance is?'

Black blew out his cheeks and lifted his hands palms upwards: at first he gave no answer, but after a moment said abruptly, 'Sit down, James, sit down.'

Feeling some surprise at the change of tone, Ogilvie sat facing the Adjutant's desk. Black got to his feet and prowled about the room, restlessly. There was silence apart from the creak of woodwork and the faint noise from the *punkahs*. Black stopped by a window, and with a sudden almost nervous movement jerked the shutters open and stared out across the parade. With his back to Ogilvie he said, 'It's all very surprising –

24

the substance. Unbelievable. I'll tell you as briefly as I can.'

He did so. Ogilvie listened intently. Black said, 'It's the Viceroy's personal order–'

'That we've been chosen for the escort?'

'No, no. That came from Murree–'

'From my father?'

'Who else?' Black's voice was sardonic: he had never forgiven Ogilvie for being the son of the father. 'Sir Iain chose us – and our brigaded battalions – the Commander-in-Chief having chosen the Northern Army in the first place. It's the Viceroy's decision that an escort be provided – for a Russian! I find it strange, James.'

'He'll have had orders from Whitehall, won't he?'

'Perhaps. Or possibly merely advice – we don't know.'

'Advice not too precisely spelled out? Diplomatic deviousness, designed to avoid blame later? Is that what you're driving at, Andrew?'

Black swung round, lips pursed. 'By no means. It's not for us to question, to ponder imponderables.'

'Yet I think that's just what you're doing, isn't it? You say it's unbelievable. Why's that?'

Black sat down, fanning himself with a hand. 'It's the involvement of Her Majesty.'

'Through the Grand Duchess?'

'Not quite that. She can't help what her granddaughter's told to do by her adopted country's masters. It's her reaction, James.'

'A perfectly proper one. The Grand Duchess is the responsibility of the Grand Duke now!'

'Oh yes, very proper. But – unlike Her Majesty.' Black paused, tapped his desk, sucked in breath, blew it out again, looking much ill-at-ease. 'I've no wish to sound disloyal, you'll appreciate that, I know, James. I'm as loyal as any subject ... but I'm bound to say that the Queen has a reputation for – for–'

'Interference in family matters, controlling all the crowned heads of Europe through marriage vows?'

'An extreme view, James. I didn't say that.' Black looked more discomfited than ever, gnawing at a trailing end of his moustache. 'I would prefer to call it taking her responsibilities seriously. Her Majesty is a strong woman, James, and forthright. Besides, as we all know, she misses the Prince Consort even now, and I think acts for him as well as for herself. I think I need say no more.'

26

'No,' Ogilvie agreed, grinning. 'I've taken your point, and it sounds a good one. There's a contradiction of character, and you wonder why.'

'Precisely.'

'It's hardly up to us. Won't it have occurred to Lord Elgin?'

'It has indeed occurred to His Excellency, and also to Sir George White, and to your father, and to–'

'Fettleworth?'

Black nodded. 'In the case of Sir Iain and General Fettleworth – rumbustiously, I gather. Your father at any rate is no respector of persons, James, and I understand he expressed himself vividly. The thing is this: no-one can do anything about it. You'll agree there.'

'The Viceroy could check–'

'No, James, not even His Excellency can suggest to Her Majesty that she has a reputation as a meddler. There is nothing to be done, and I mention it only because I feel there is something else behind it all, something we have not been told. Perhaps I should not have spoken so freely.' Black's hands were shaking a little; he gave the appearance of a man back-peddling hard, fearful that the Queen herself might be eavesdropping outside the door, having by some magic means arrived for his personal discomfiture from Windsor Castle. 'We shall say no more about it, James. The reason I wished to speak to you was purely regimental–'

'Oh? What have I done now, Andrew?'

'Not a reprimand,' Black said stiffly. 'Orders. During the forthcoming operation – the escort, that is – your company will perform special duties. As I told you, the brigade as a whole will be relieved below Dehra Dun by a fresh column out of Meerut, but you and your company are to continue into Nepal. It is a compliment, I gather ... you are regarded as an experienced officer.' Black sounded grudging on the point. 'In the meantime, having met the Grand Duchess at Jamrud, and having accompanied the brigade on the march south of Peshawar, you will, when so ordered by the Brigadier-General, march ahead of the column to act as an advanced party – as scouts to prepare the way and deal with any trouble you may find before Her Imperial Highness becomes involved. You understand, James?'

'Yes. How far ahead?'

Black said, 'You'll be expected to maintain

a distance of around five miles from the van of the column at all times, and to keep four-hourly contact by means of runners and the heliograph. The Grand Duchess herself will travel in the palanquin, carried by Russians–'

'And the Cossacks?'

'They will form the close-escort for the palanquin.'

'Guns?'

Black nodded. 'The brigade will take a mountain battery but no field guns.'

'Cavalry?'

'No cavalry as such beyond the Cossacks, but there will be the normal complement of horses appropriate to an infantry brigade, of course, plus mules for the supply column, which will include medical stores, detached from Division.' Black coughed. 'For my part, in addition to my duties as Adjutant, I shall, since the 114th is the senior regiment in terms of Indian service, act as Brigade Major–'

'What about Major Hay?'

'The Colonel prefers to retain him as second-in-command,' Black said, stiff once again: Ogilvie kept his face blank. The Colonel, should he become a casualty, would by no means wish to see command of the battalion pass to Black, that was certain, for Black had an extraordinary ability to antagonise both officers and other ranks. With Black as Brigade Major there would in any case be fireworks on the march ... Black went on, formally now, 'It is my hope that I shall have your complete co-operation, Captain Ogilvie. I need not remind you, I am sure, of the importance of the success of the escort—'

'Nor of my duty,' Ogilvie interrupted.

'I shall hope not. In the meantime, you will be good enough to exercise your company in their duties as extended scouts. I shall expect heliograph practice among other things, also a full awareness among all ranks of what will be expected of them on the march and a full knowledge of the terrain with particular reference to conditions inside Nepal – which your own detachment will need to be familiar with as they approach Katmandu. I realise none of us has experience of Nepal, but Brigade will provide you with all the information you will need. In addition, there will be Political Officers joining you with the column out of Meerut, and they'll be in a position to advise you further.' Black pulled out his watch. 'You are expected at Brigade for a full briefing at two o'clock.'

Ogilvie nodded, and started to rise. 'Is that all?'

'For now, yes. Oh, just one more thing: I shall be seeing all other company commanders and senior N.C.O.s after luncheon, and I shall tell you now what I shall tell them then. We are acting as escort to a princess of the blood, no matter that she's married to a Russian. There will be no foul language. There will be no sights unfit for a lady to see – urination upon the march will be performed–'

'By numbers?'

Black's face darkened. 'Kindly do not be impertinent, Captain Ogilvie! Will be performed, if I might be allowed to finish, *circumspectly*. Clothing will be at all times clean and decent and properly worn. Badges and buttons will be polished. Neckbands will not be loosened without express permission from me. Filthy soldiers' songs will not be sung. Men will not...'

The list, petulantly given almost as though disobedience was expected in advance, was endless. Crossing the parade back to the Mess for luncheon, James Ogilvie wondered if the Adjutant could be angling for a K.C.V.O. awarded for a smart turn-out even if the Grand Duchess Sergius should succumb to an unsmart and smelly enemy given his chance by men with bladders too painfully extended for straight shooting.

In the early morning three weeks later the brigade, consisting of the 114th Highlanders, the 2nd Border Regiment, and the 2nd York and Lancasters with their support tail moved out of cantonments for the mouth of the Khyber Pass, marching to the skirl of pipes, the beat of drums, the wailing of the English battalions' fifes and the thunder of the depot brass, advancing in column of route past the prideful swell of General Fettleworth's stomach, scarlet-garbed, as he stood at the salute with his Chief of Staff a respectful distance behind. Ahead of the long column, immediately before the trundling mule-borne guns of the mountain battery, rode the Brigadier-General in command, Hilary Margesson, late the Grenadier Guards, a man of frankly small experience of the hill tribes but chosen by Fettleworth on account of his past associations and his links with royalty forged by service in the Household Brigade: his would be a familiar manner to any British-born princess, to whom a touch of old times would be welcome enough after the gruelling trek from Kabul. The Brigadier-General sat his horse splendidly: he was a tall man with piercing blue eyes and a heavy grey moustache, his back as straight as that of a young hussar, his khaki-drill tunic immaculately starched and looking crisp despite the climbing sun. Later, when the column had moved out of Peshawar, much sweat darkened the jacket of Andrew Black as he rode up and down the line of the Royal Strathspeys, his sharp eye critical of dress and precision as the step was maintained to the beat of the drums. It was a hot day's march: the neckbands sat around the soldiers' necks like damp pudding, fiendishly uncomfortable until, after a word from the Colonel, Black grudgingly passed the order to march at ease. He accompanied this relaxation with a reminder that next day, when in company with the Grand Duchess, they would be smartened up again.

That evening the column was halted and the men pitched tents by companies, with some eight miles yet to march the following morning to Jamrud and the rendezvous. Ogilvie with his subalterns walked down the line of tents when camp had been made, stopping for a word here and there; and before the sun went down all officers were summoned to sit in a semi-circle facing the Brigade H.Q. tent while the Chief of Staff delivered a final briefing, reminding his audience that the escort would last for close upon 450 miles through difficult country to Dehra Dun, until the column marching north from Meerut made contact.

At 3.45 a.m. the sentries guarding the perimeter of the encampment heard the far distant sound of heavy gunfire, coming apparently from inside the Khyber: Margesson and the battalion commanders were awakened by the officer of the guard, and the Brigadier-General ordered the men roused out. As the first faint streaks of dawn began to lighten the sky to the east beyond Peshawar, camp was hastily struck. The column was reformed for forced-marching to Jamrud behind the pipes and drums of the Royal Strathspeys, with scouts above them on the hillsides as they came into the frowning highlands extending out from the mouth of the pass.

Chapter 3

There was no more gunfire: the Chief of Staff, Colonel Maurice, was of the opinion that a mere skirmish had been in progress.

'A handful of tribesmen trying their luck,' he suggested to Margesson.

'To be repulsed by field guns, Colonel?'

Maurice shrugged. 'A sledgehammer to crack a nut, sir – perhaps. But considering the value of the cargo ... the Cossacks will be taking no chances.'

Margesson, reining in his horse and halting the column, stared for a while through field-glasses, surveying the cleft in the hills and Fort Jamrud perched distantly upon its rocky crag. A few minutes later, as if in answer to his unspoken thoughts, a heliograph began flashing, reflecting the early sun's rays in a message to Brigade.

Margesson turned, a hand resting on his horse's rump. 'Signaller!' he called.

'Sir!' Running up, the man saluted then

began reading, repeating the message aloud for another signaller to write down. 'Russian party one mile west. No request made for assistance but propose giving cover from fort.' The signaller glanced up at the Brigadier-General. 'Sir! The message ends.'

Margesson nodded briefly, still scanning the entry to the pass. After a moment he brought down his field-glasses and snapped them back into the leather case hanging from his shoulder. Turning once more, he lifted a hand towards the Colonel of the Royal Strathspeys, and Lord Dornoch rode his horse forward.

'Sir?'

'I shall not move the whole brigade in, Dornoch. Kindly detach a company of yours to march ahead to meet the Grand Duchess.'

'Yes, sir.'

'And send a bugler. The proper compliments to be paid, if you please.'

'Yes, sir. And – the pipes?'

Margesson laughed. 'If you must, Colonel, if you must! Take care, however, that they do not scare the life out of our charge–'

'Sir, Her Imperial Highness will no doubt have stayed at Balmoral–'

'Where Her Majesty's piper will have put

her off her breakfast porridge I don't doubt.
But I take your point, Colonel, and you
mustn't take me too seriously!' He laughed
again. 'By all means, the pipes and drums.'

Dornoch saluted and turned back to
Black. 'Pass the word for Captain Ogilvie, if
you please, Captain Black, and for Pipe-
Major Ross. B Company is to detach to the
mouth of the pass and form vanguard and
rearguard, the pipes and drums leading.'

Nearing the Khyber's mouth, James Ogilvie
looked up at the high-perched fort and the
gleaming bayonets caught by the sun atop
the walls, the bayonets of the Khyber Rifles.
Colour-Sergeant MacTrease brought his
attention down again to ground level.

'Sir, the Russkies.' MacTrease pointed:
ahead horsemen were coming into view,
rounding a massive rock outcrop below Fort
Jamrud. Visible from time to time behind
the Cossack riders was a curtained palanquin, lurching over the terrible track in the
grip of four uniformed men. 'The Grand
Duchess'll be in yon handcart, no doubt
sir?'

Ogilvie grinned. 'Right, Colour-Sar'nt,
but I wouldn't use that term in the Russian's hearing. They may be touchy!'

'Will they speak English, sir?'

'I don't doubt their officers will.' Ogilvie turned to his senior subaltern, Henry Stonehouse. 'Your half-company in the van,' he said, 'Mr Matheson's in rear. Pipe-Major?'

'Sir?'

'I shall lead the pipes and drums, Pipe-Major. When I give the order, the bugler sounds off.'

'Aye, sir. What'll be the pipers' tune, sir?'

'Frankly, I'm damned if I know!' Ogilvie said with a laugh. 'It should be one of the National Anthems, British or Russian, but I doubt if they'll cope with either!' He paused. 'We'll settle for "Riobain Gorm nan Granndach".'

' "The Grant's Blue Ribbon", sir, aye.' The Pipe-Major saluted and turned away, marching towards his pipers. B Company, under the orders of the subalterns of half-companies, divided, two sections marching on to wheel off the track ready to come up in rear of the Cossack escort, two sections falling out and re-forming beside the track behind Ogilvie and the pipes and drummers. With considerable interest Ogilvie watched the approach of the Russians: it was a dramatic enough picture against the background of the Khyber hills. The Cossacks, men born to the saddle and to arms, were of splendid physique, tall and bearded and with the faces of traditional warriors beneath tall fur helmets, legs encased in high leather boots and great curved scimitar-like weapons hanging from their horses' equipment. Each man also carried a long-barrelled rifle held across the saddle-cloth in front of his body. The Cossacks rode on, their faces haughty, giving no word of greeting. There were two squadrons ahead of the palanquin, two more with the guns in rear, plus what appeared to be a company of infantry marching on the flanks: these foot-soldiers no doubt formed the bearers for the palanquin. In addition there was a straggling supply-train of heavily laden mules and wagons. The palanquin itself was a magnificent affair with a gilded wooden canopy surmounted by the replica of a crown, and silken side hangings, now tight-drawn. Ogilvie stared in wonder as the palanquin was borne closer along the track: he found it hard to believe that behind those silken curtains was the granddaughter of the Queen-Empress herself, thus strangely proceeding out of the terrible Khyber Pass...

He almost let the palanquin go by without

the proper respects; it was Pipe-Major Ross who nudged him back to his duties. 'Sir, the bugler.'

'By God ... Bugler – royal salute!'

The notes came out, stridently bursting into the crisp air. Ogilvie's drawn claymore came up in personal salute as the two sections of the Highlanders presented arms. Then air was puffed into the pipes, and a few bars of "The Grants' Blue Ribbon", traditionally played by the Royal Strathspeys for inspecting officers, crashed out to echo off the rocky hillsides. The Russian officer commanding the escort returned the salute punctiliously but coldly, with an almost contemptuous look. There was no response from the palanquin. The escort rode on, looking neither to right nor left. Ogilvie's reaction was one of embarrassment and some cold anger: he was not accustomed to seeing the British Army virtually disregarded. He brought his claymore down from the salute and caught his subaltern's eye. Formally, his face red, he snapped, 'Form escort, if you please, Mr Stonehouse. Pipe-Major, the pipes and drums in the van, to march at rest.'

'Sir!'

Ogilvie looked to the rear, where Second

Lieutenant Matheson was now coming along with the rest of B Company. Ogilvie spurred his horse and rode eastwards along the track, catching up with the Russian cavalry officer and reining in his horse to ride alongside as Stonehouse's half-company doubled past.

'Captain Ogilvie,' he said, 'of Her Majesty's 114th Highlanders, at your service, sir.'

The Russian gave him a quick sideways glance. 'Colonel Count Tomislav, of the First Cossack Regiment of the Imperial Bodyguard.' He spoke good English.

'You are welcome to British India, sir.'

The reply was a mere inclination of the head. Then the Russian asked coldly, 'You are here to escort us, Captain?'

'As far as the main body of my column, which you can see ahead.'

'Its strength?'

'A brigade. We take you as far as Dehra Dun, then a fresh column takes over to Katmandu,' Ogilvie paused. 'And – Her Imperial Highness, the Grand Duchess Sergius?'

'What of her?'

Ogilvie was nettled by the tone. 'She is a princess of our own royal house–'

'No longer, Captain. Now she is Russian.'

'Yes indeed.' Ogilvie coughed. 'Even so, I

would have expected a sight of her, sir – with respect, an acknowledgement of courtesies–'

'Her Imperial Highness,' the Cossack interrupted harshly, 'is unwell. She wishes not to be disturbed, Captain.'

'I see. I trust she'll soon be fit again. We have doctors–'

'So have we. Her Imperial Highness is in excellent hands. *You* need have no concern on her account.'

The manner was rude, overbearing. Count Tomislav, keeping his eyes front, rode on in silence. After a few moments Ogilvie touched his spurs to his horse and moved ahead, taking up a position in the lead of the silent pipes and drums. As they closed the column he increased the distance between himself and the Russians, riding in to report to Brigade. He found Lord Dornoch and Andrew Black, together with the other regimental colonels, grouped with the Brigadier-General. He made his report, adding that the Russian officer seemed resentful of interference.

'Does he, by jove?' Margesson said. 'We were requested by his own Court, but I suppose it's his privilege to feel slighted – they're proud buggers, these Cossacks!' He paused. 'What's up with the Grand Duchess?'

'Count Tomislav didn't say, sir.'

Margesson chuckled. 'Seasick, I shouldn't wonder, being trundled around in that mobile four-poster bed! Poor woman, she has the devil of a way to go still. In the circumstances,' he added to his Chief of Staff, 'we'll have no more formalities. I'll simply make myself known to the Russian, and then if he doesn't want to rest his men we'll form column and move straight out.'

Count Tomislav required no rest: there was scarcely a pause as formally he returned the Brigadier-General's greeting. Column was formed with a certain lack of dignity as the Royal Strathspeys hastened to take up their position in the van with the Border Regiment as rearguard and the York and Lancasters spread out to guard the flanks. Andrew Black's harrying voice could be heard continually and loudly, overriding the shouts of the colour-sergeants and the corporals: he was in a bad temper and so was the Colonel, like Ogilvie unaccustomed to being slighted. Rumour had it that the Brigadier-General was seething also: he had been permitted no exchange with the Grand

Duchess whom, with his Grenadier tradition, he regarded almost as his own property and damnation to the Russians. For a while, as the brigade marched to head to the south of Peshawar, the air had been more or less discretely blue, the venom uttered in tones that would not reach Count Tomislav. But the word spread and the rank-and-file grinned gleefully behind their hands, certain that there would be fireworks before long. However, when the combined column halted for luncheon, the Brigadier-General made an effort and approached Count Tomislav as the latter dismounted to sit before a damask-covered table in an ornate arm-chair lifted from a commissariat cart by two Russian soldiers.

'We heard firing from the Khyber earlier, Count Tomislav. I trust you had no trouble.

Tomislav waved a hand. 'No trouble.'

'Ah. A Pathan foray, a skirmish?'

'A little thing. My artillery dealt with them.'

'How?'

The Russian stared, shrugged. 'My guns blew the natives to pieces, that is all. I had but two dead, two common soldiers only.'

'I see. You buried them, of course.'

'I did not.'

'You didn't?' Margesson's eyes bulged: even if not long on the Frontier, he knew that a British regiment always buried its dead. 'You know, I suppose, what will happen to them, Count Tomislav?'

'No, I do not know,' Tomislav answered distantly and without interest: luncheon was coming up from his field kitchen, and he was hungry. The deaths of common soldiers were of small account. He watched a stream of cooks and orderlies bringing salmon from a heavily insulated ice-box, a convenience that could scarcely last much longer, fruit, bottles of good wine from France, also ice-packed ... Brigadier-General Margesson looked on in amazement: his own table would not be meanly garnished, but this was field luxury on the grand scale, and he proceeded, with relish, to wreck it.

'Pathan women will come out,' he said loudly, 'and hack off their genitals. These they will cram into their mouths, the lips of which will be sewn up over them.'

He watched Count Tomislav. The Russian smiled, picked up a silver fork and delicately separated a segment of salmon flesh, impaled a succulent-looking circle of cucumber, and munched with enjoyment. Laying the fork down before the next mouthful, he wiped lips and moustache with a clean linen napkin and looked up at the Brigadier-General. 'Genitals, genitals,' he said dismissingly. 'They are no use to a dead man – or to an ageing one either, General, do you not agree? Do not bother me with genitals.' He resumed eating. Margesson turned on his heel and walked away, passing the guarded palanquin where two women, ladies in waiting no doubt, oddities to find upon a march, were handing luncheon through the curtains. The Grand Duchess was faring as well as Count Tomislav: Margesson didn't grudge her the privilege. Her journey was not one for any woman, let alone a princess of the blood, and any easing of it was welcome enough. But he felt, and felt strongly, that manners demanded a greeting. The food going into the palanquin scarcely, he thought, supported the story of a woman too sick to bestow a word upon her British escort. Margesson paused in his stride, frowning, pulling at his moustache. Becoming aware of Lord Dornoch in the vicinity he called to him.

'A word, Colonel.'

'Sir?'

The Brigadier-General nodded towards the palanquin. 'What would you do?'

'I'd observe Russian customs, I fancy.'

'You would, would you?' Margesson frowned again. 'What are they – d'you know?'

Dornoch smiled. 'I'm afraid I don't. Not knowing, I'd play safe, General. I'm sure the Grand Duchess will send for you as soon as she's ready.'

'Well – perhaps you're right ... perhaps you're right! But it's damned queer all the same, Dornoch. I've commanded a battalion of Guards ... I've done the palace guard, the London season – all those damned debutantes – I've met Her Majesty times without number! Levées, garden parties, tea parties even – bunfights! You'd think the granddaughter would be only too pleased to see someone from London, wouldn't you, sick or not?'

Dornoch said thoughtfully, 'Yes, it's a point, General.'

'Your young Ogilvie. How did he take it?'

'He was surprised, but more at the manner of the Russians than of the invisible Grand Duchess, I fancy!'

'Ah-ha. A funny bunch, like all damned foreigners, and as for Count Tomislav, the fellow's nothing but a barbarian, and a well-fed one too.'

'Sir?'

Margesson explained about the genitals, and then, nodding once more towards the heavily-guarded palanquin, said, 'D'you know, Dornoch, I may be starting hares, but I'm not happy.'

'Can you be more precise?' Dornoch asked.

'Yes, I can.' The Brigadier-General lowered his voice, which had tended to rise with his emotions. 'It may not be Her Imperial Highness in that damned cart. The Russians may be fooling us all! Don't ask me why, I need time to make an appreciation of the possibilities. Until I've done so – not a word to a soul, Colonel.'

'Very good, sir.' Dornoch saluted, and made to move away, but was stopped by the Brigadier-General.

'A moment, Colonel. The extended scouting company, Ogilvie's company. According to my orders, they were to move ahead once we were east of the Indus–'

'A fair distance yet–'

'Yes indeed. There is no need for a decision yet, but I may change the orders to keep Ogilvie's company with us. You never know,' Margesson added darkly, and turned away towards his own luncheon.

★ ★ ★

'A word in your ear, Captain Ogilvie.'

'By all means, Captain Black.' Ogilvie glanced sideways as the Adjutant rode up, lips thin beneath the harsh hairs of the moustache. After the meal, hastily taken and somewhat scanty in regard to the men, the column had resumed the march under burnished skies. Sweat ran freely down exposed skin, soaked into tunics and kilts, causing the latter to swing damply and heavily around the knees of the Highlanders. 'What is it?'

'Your company. They are slack, man, slack!'

'Only mine?'

'Kindly do not be impertinent!' Black snapped. 'God knows, I have a difficult enough task. Don't make it worse.'

'I'm sorry.' Ogilvie stifled a sigh. 'Can you describe this slackness?'

'Slovenly marching, talking in the ranks, blind eyes being turned by the N.C.O.s more often than not.' Black was almost ticking off the list of sins on his fingers. 'Kilts at an incorrect distance from the knee. One man, who I could not identify, made a vulgar noise after I had ridden past–'

'I'll smarten them up,' Ogilvie said. The

Adjutant was, after all, the Adjutant.

'Please do. If there are any more vulgar noises, Captain Ogilvie, and the man cannot be identified, then I shall have the whole of B Company on a charge of dumb insolence!'

'Very well, Captain Black.'

Black sniffed. 'Take my advice,' he said, 'and make a start on your colour-sergeant. The man's too indifferent for words.'

'I disagree—'

'Then disagree by all means, but keep your disagreement to yourself and do as you are told.'

Black rode on briskly, making towards the Colonel at the battalion's head. Ogilvie bit down hard on his rising temper, turned in the saddle to look along the line of marching Scots. It went without saying that in his view the Royal Strathspeys were peerless: the regiment was in his bones, in his blood, was woven deep into the fabric of his very life, was in basis a family affair. His father had commanded before his elevation to the General Staff; before him, *his* father. In the fullness of time James Ogilvie hoped to command in his turn: that currently was the peak of his ambition, though he realised that time might give him further targets. The regiment was his pride and he was as jealous for its reputation and smartness as was Andrew Black. But in his approach he differed fundamentally from the Adjutant. Black, though a Scot, had been brought up in England, so had previous generations: there was much money in the Black family, money made in steel and also inherited from steel, for marriage alliances had been made with the great Bessemer steel family. But English money failed to compensate for lack of Scots awareness – awareness that Scots of all ranks had an independence of mind and spirit that no Englishman could ever fully understand. They were not insubordinate but they were prideful: they could not be harried. Bred into them almost unawares were the ancient traditions of the clans, the clans where every man except for the chief himself had been equal within the clan, a system that in a very positive sense had arrived at communism centuries before Karl Marx. This, Black would never comprehend if he lived a thousand years. He would never understand that the drooping kilt upon the march, the occasional loosened neckband against orders, the vulgar noise behind the rigid back of authority – these were the mild exhibitions of inbred independence, the only ones permissible within an army's discipline, and a Scots-bred officer knew them to be the safety-valves. Thus within limits they were respected: the N.C.O.s knew very precisely, and much better than did Black, when to turn the blind eye. When the fighting started, the Scots rallied: that was what mattered.

Ogilvie sighed again, and, turning his horse, moved out of the line of advance to remain motionless beside the track and watch the battalion march by. He was given one or two sardonic looks: the men would have seen him being approached by the Adjutant. As the rear files of B Company went past, he called to MacTrease.

'Colour-Sar'nt, fall out if you please.'

'Sir!' MacTrease doubled of the track, saluting and looking up at Ogilvie.

'Colour MacTrease, I advise you to be watchful on the march. We're not on the parade, but we have ladies with us, as you know.'

'Aye, sir. They'll be safe enough, sir, I'll warrant.'

Ogilvie smiled. 'I'm not speaking of the enemy now, nor even of any hot blood among the men! A certain smartness,

Colour MacTrease – that's the order of the day. Do you understand me?'

'Aye, sir.' There was a grin on the Colour-Sergeant's leathery face, a look of mischief mixed with total understanding. 'We want no *black* marks in B Company, sir, is that it?'

Ogilvie could not restrain an answering grin of his own. 'Off with you, Colour-Sar'nt! Let's hear that farmyard voice of yours!'

'Sir!' MacTrease about-turned smartly and doubled ahead to catch up the rear of his company. Lightly Ogilvie touched his spurs to his horse's flanks and moved up the column after MacTrease. He listened to the raised voice, the smart orders to the drill-sergeants and corporals, the careful lack of any obscenity that might carry to the lumbering palanquin being borne along behind the Scots and ahead of the men from the Border lands of England. A moment later the latter's fifes and drums started up, a stirring and cheerful sound that made men's feet lighter on the stony, sun-hard ground. On an impulse Ogilvie once again pulled his horse out of the advance, and waited beside the track as the palanquin moved up in the hands of its bearers behind the close screen of Russian riders. Ahead of the concealed Grand Duchess rode Colonel Count Tomislav, gaunt and tall on his horse, his expression seeming still contemptuous of the British infantry. As he went past he glanced at Ogilvie, bowed his head in a sardonic movement, and smiled. Ogilvie noticed the long yellow teeth, like the fangs of a vampire, and felt a sudden shaft of pity for the Englishwoman committed to this man's care on a long and dangerous journey. As he waited for the passage of the palanquin and its escort, he was aware of Count Tomislav looking back at him enquiringly. Disregarding the Russian, he stared at the richly embroidered curtains as the hand-borne vehicle went by. Those curtains were still tightly drawn, and Ogilvie had the impression that a hand was clasped round the join, holding them tighter: yet at the same time he had another impression, a strong one, that he was in fact being watched from some chink where the two curtains met.

Turning his horse again, he cantered up beside the column and took up his position in the advance on Dehra Dun.

Chapter 4

The speed of the fleet was that of the slowest ship: the palanquin could not be borne at full infantry pace even though the bearers were changed at frequent intervals. Thus it was not until the ninth day after the rendezvous below Fort Jamrud that the column dropped down between Rawalpindi and Kohat with the fording of the Jhelum River, tributary of the great Indus, still some six or seven more days ahead. Ogilvie's company still marched with the main advance. By this time a curious, inexplicable sense of unease had pervaded the whole column even though so far the advance had been peaceful and unimpeded by so much as a single sniper's bullet from the mountain crags rearing above the passes as the long, trailing caravan wound its way through behind the scouting parties and pickets provided by the various regiments in turn.

Black, in the course of his duties as

Brigade Major, became aware of the uneasy feeling and remarked upon it to Lord Dornoch in bivouacs after the bugles had blown for supper on the evening of that ninth day of march.

'It's due,' Dornoch said as he puffed at his pipe, 'to the mystery surrounding that closed palanquin.'

'I agree, Colonel.'

'Has *anyone* seen the Grand Duchess?'

Black said, 'Not to my knowledge, Colonel, no.' He paused. 'I feel I should report to the Brigadier-General.'

Dornoch glanced up. 'Report what, Andrew?'

'That the men appear anxious.'

'Yes,' Dornoch said, 'I think you should.' He said no more; Margesson, after all, had enjoined him to silence as to certain worries about the palanquin's occupant. Black saluted and made off. After a while the Colonel got to his feet and, still puffing meditatively at his pipe, ambled alone down the line of men resting beside the track under the watchful eyes of sentries posted on the hillsides in roughly-constructed sangars. The sun was going down now into the short Indian twilight, and a breeze was stirring cold and fresh out of Himalaya to the north. Already some of the men, having eaten the frugal supper provided by the field-kitchens, were huddled into thick blankets, their rifles ready by their sides: taking all the ease they could before, once again, the early-morning bugles roused them out. Dornoch, helmetless and with his tunic unbuttoned, walked with a hand in the pocket of his tartan trews, clear indication that he had no desire for weary men to get up and stand at attention. Moving on beyond his own battalion line, he came to the men of the York and Lancaster Regiment, queuing at their field-kitchen with their mess-tins, rifles slung from their shoulders in the instant readiness for action that was not only orders but also instinct on the part of all soldiers serving on the North-West Frontier.

Dornoch came abreast of the palanquin, laid down now on a wide, flat rock surface, with an armed and dismounted Cossack on guard at each corner – like a guard of honour, Dornoch thought, motionless beside a catafalque at the lying-in-state of a dead sovereign. It was a weird scene in that wild terrain below the mountain peaks, with the wind, stronger already, whining through the darkening pass: Dornoch could well understand a degree of tension in the men, his own Scots especially. Always Scots had had their quality of feyness, even the dourest, most prosaic of them – and among Scots, those from the highlands were the most prone of all to feyness. Slowly Dornoch walked on, almost feeling the stares of the Cossacks as a physical force. Before he had moved far, he heard a sound from the palanquin: a very faint sound, like a woman's sob, and then weeping, quickly stifled. He stopped in his tracks, his fists clenching in his pockets, face darkening like the surrounding hills. He glanced at the Cossack guards: impassively, they stared back – stared as though challenging him to interfere. There were no further sounds, and Dornoch walked on, his heart thudding. He scarcely knew what his duty might be: if there was a suffering, unhappy woman, granddaughter of the Queen-Empress, in that palanquin, then would it not be considered the duty of a British officer to help in some way? But the Grand Duchess was Russian now, in the hands of an armed escort of her own adopted country, an escort no doubt approved not only by the Czar of All the Russias but by her husband the Grand Duke Sergius. It was not strictly

Dornoch's business, and the escort would react to any act of interference as they would take it to be: the resulting implications would rock Government House and the Viceroy, who had promised not interference but assistance; the tides of trouble would wash from Calcutta across the seas to Whitehall and Windsor ... Dornoch gave himself a shake, and moved on along the rocky pass. Women were apt to weep for divers reasons, not all of them sensible ones ... Dornoch smiled to himself: his own dear wife wept on birthdays, invariably – his own, hers, their children's. Women were unpredictable and currently the Russians, for so long looked upon with high suspicion along the North-West Frontier, were friends and allies – or so, it seemed, authority had decided!

Lost in his thoughts, Dornoch almost jumped when a voice hailed from the shadows.

'Good evening, sir.'

'Oh – it's you, Major!'

Major Waring, second-in-command of the York and Lancasters, came away from his background of rock. 'I startled you, sir – I'm sorry.'

'I would never confess to being startled,'

Dornoch said gravely, but with a twinkle in his eye. 'Not that this place isn't somewhat spectral!'

'No more so than Glencoe.'

'You know Glencoe?'

Waring laughed. 'I had a MacDonald ancestor on the distaff side – I made a pilgrimage, once. It's a long haul by bicycle from Fort William, but well worth while. It was a fine, sunny day, and Loch Leven was splendid, unbelievable. Then I came back along the pass as dusk was falling.' He paused, some odd quality in his voice. ' *"Oh, cruel is the snow that sweeps Glencoe, and covers the grave o' Donald ... Oh, cruel were the foe that raped Glencoe, and murdered the house of MacDonald"*. Yes, I found it – impressive.'

'Impressive enough to remember, Major?'

'You can't get away from it out here,' Waring answered, and gave a sudden shiver. 'No snow in this season – but the wind's chilly, sir.'

'Yes, indeed. But – the palanquin's well curtained against it.'

'Sir?' Waring sounded surprised.

'Your curiosity not been aroused, Major?'

Waring shrugged. 'Ours not to reason why ... but yes, I suppose it has. The Queen's granddaughter, after all! The Russians do seem overly sensitive and possessive, and I've heard the men wondering, certainly.'

'What's your theory, then?'

'Oh, I haven't one really, I just do my duty!' Waring laughed. 'If I have a theory at all, well, I suppose it's just that the Russians regard her as their business and see no reason to be forthcoming to us.'

'You may be right, Major.' Dornoch paused. 'As I passed the palanquin just now, I heard crying.'

'Did you indeed?' The Major seemed concerned, but after a moment added, 'It's a hard journey for a woman, and she's far from home.'

'All the more reason for her to wish to see a friendly face. There's duress around somewhere!'

Waring shrugged. 'Duress and the Russians appear, historically, to go together.'

'Have you seen her?' Dornoch asked abruptly.

'Seen her, sir?'

'She can't be confined to the palanquin twenty-four hours a day.'

'No. Oh, I've caught a glimpse, but that's all. The thunderbox, you know – dammit, she's human! She goes off the track surrounded by her women, and the Cossacks

61

maintaining a sort of extended screen.' Waring looked at Dornoch with curiosity. 'Why d'you ask, sir?'

'Just a thought,' Dornoch answered quietly, the glow from his pipe-bowl striking a brief redness from his features. He bade Waring a goodnight and turned away, walking back to his own regimental line of bivouacs, knocking out his pipe as full dark came down. Passing the palanquin again he heard no further sounds but was acutely aware of the presence of the Cossack guard, of their hands ready around the triggers of their rifles. As he came, somewhat thankfully, back to the Royal Strathspeys' sector of the pass, he saw ahead the ramrod figure of the Regimental Sergeant-Major standing on some rising ground. Cunningham was wearing his Highland bonnet and, with that and his kilt silhouetted against a climbing moon, he looked for all the world like the soldier atop the Black Watch memorial in Aberfeldy in far-off Perthshire. Seeing the approach of the Colonel, the R.S.M. jumped down, a nimble movement for a man of his size, and slammed to the salute.

'All quiet, Sar'nt-Major?' Dornoch asked.

'All quiet, sir. I think we have too much strength, sir, for the tribes to take a risk.'

'Rubbish, Sar'nt-Major, and well you know it!' Dornoch laughed. 'I've never known them scared of numbers in the passes before! We'll not relax our guard.'

'We'll not do that, sir. I've spoken personally to the sentries, sir, though there was no real need. They know well who we have with us and they'll be alert as never before, you have my word on it, sir.'

'Thank you, Mr Cunningham.' Lord Dornoch moved on toward his own bivouac, his tent and sleeping-bag laid out by his native bearer in a cleft between two rocky outcrops where he would be as protected as possible against the cold night wind. Around him the remains of the evening meal were being cleared away in the dark, no lights showing to act as targets for lurking snipers on the heights, the fires of the field-kitchens doused now that they had done their work of heating soup and water. There was some quiet conversation but no shouting, no songs: as ever, night bivouacs in hill country were the times of greatest danger. So far they had been lucky: along the way they had seen the customary surveillance maintained upon any body of British troops on the march – the tattered, warlike figures on the crests, watchful behind the jezails; but that was all. Dornoch pondered on likely reasons: luck was not something to be militarily relied upon or even to take into account when assessing possibilities. There was some other factor, and it could well be to do with the Russians, though God alone knew why: some form of bribery would be the most tenable answer if collusion were indeed the case.

That night, Dornoch slept but little. In such fitful sleep as came to him he suffered vivid nightmares in which he heard desperate sobbing coming again from the guarded palanquin.

'Sahib, sahib.' The bearer's voice was loud and urgent as he bent over the Colonel, who did not stir. The native tried again, more loudly: he laid no hands upon the Colonel Sahib, for such were the British orders. British officers, roused from sleep, could react in bad temper and lash out at native bearers, and that would never do. 'Colonel Sahib, wake please!'

The urgency penetrated: Lord Dornoch sat up suddenly. 'What is it, man?'

'Sahib, it is the Brigadier-General Sahib–'

'What's happened?' Already Dornoch had reached for his revolver and was coming out of the sleeping-bag into the first of the dawn.

'Sahib, nothing has happened. The Brigadier-General Sahib sends word to all Commanding Officers and to the Brigade Major Sahib. He sends his compliments and asks for their attendance, Colonel Sahib.'

'When? Now?'

'Yes, Colonel Sahib.'

'All right,' Dornoch said irritably, and waved his hand. Salaaming, the bearer backed away, then took to his heels. Dornoch rose and stretched, sniffing the keen air, looking up at the high peaks, some of the highest still streaked with the remnants of last winter's snows, searching automatically for the wild figures of watching tribesmen, finding none and seeing only the extended pickets of the regiments. Checking his revolver, Dornoch thrust it back into its holster, which he strapped on. Unwashed and unshaven he made his way towards the Brigadier-General's bivouac, falling in with Black on the way.

He nodded. 'Good morning, Andrew. What's all this about, d'you know?'

'I do not, Colonel, but I suspect the Brigadier-General is anxious about the Grand Duchess.'

'I think we all are,' Dornoch said. He left
it at that, and they walked on in silence,
listening to the bugles now blowing Rev-
eille, watching dog-tired men turn out to
another long day's march under what would
so soon be a cruelly burning sun. They
found Margesson impatiently striding up
and down, already beautifully turned out as
befitted a former Guards officer. Greeting
Dornoch and Black somewhat perfunc-
torily, he carried on with his restless pacing
until the Colonels of the Border Regiment
and the York and Lancasters came hurrying
up. After that he wasted no time. Though
he and his senior officers were in an isolated group by themselves, he kept his voice
down.

'Well, gentlemen,' he said. 'I'll come
directly to the point. I'm worried about the
Grand Duchess and I dare say you all know
why. The whole thing's damned odd and
I'm positive the Viceroy never envisaged
such anonymity. Yes, Dornoch?'

'Last night, General, I heard crying coming from the palanquin.'

'Crying, h'm? Sounds of distress – were
they?'

'There was no doubt about that,' Dornoch
answered with a touch of irritation. He

explained in more detail, referring also to his conversation with Major Waring.

Thoughtfully, the Brigadier-General rasped at his neat moustache. 'What do *you* make of it all?'

The question was a general one, and the answers were vague. Margesson snapped, 'If you haven't any ideas, I *have*. It seems to me to come down to two possibilities: either Her Imperial Highness is being brought by force, against her will – in which case the Russian aims are unlikely to be in the best of British interests – or she's not ruddy well there at all!'

'An impostor, sir?' Black asked, staring.

'Impostor's not quite the word, Brigade Major. Whoever she is, she'll be well enough authenticated by the Russians! Let's say she's a substitute, a dummy – a stand-in. If so – why? Who among the Russians is the real emissary, and again, why? What are they after?'

Dornoch said, 'As to your first question, General, I'd assume the supposed presence of the Grand Duchess would be the bait to gain both British approval of the journey, and a British escort. As to the rest...' He threw up his hands. 'Only Calcutta and Whitehall could answer, I suspect.'

'I doubt if they can either – though I only wish to God I could contact Government House and get myself a positive directive in the fresh circumstances! As it is, we must improvise.' Margesson turned away, and started pacing again. After a minute he turned back to the waiting officers. 'I've given this a good deal of thought, of course, and I can't disguise an element of risk. But we have to see the lady – that's vital in my opinion. We mustn't forget her birth, gentlemen. I intend making a perfectly reasonable request to the Colonel of Cossacks. It may succeed, or it may not. My view is that it will not, judging from my previous encounters with Count Tomislav.'

'And if it does not?'

Margesson blew out his cheeks. 'At the risk of repeating myself, I stress the royal relationship. If anything untoward should happen to Her Majesty's granddaughter, then I, and all of you, gentlemen, will have our careers cut short to end our days in sober reflection in Cheltenham or Bath. I have no desire for such a death in life. There will be an accident.'

The officers stared. Dornoch asked, 'An accident, General?'

'The palanquin will be overturned –

gently if possible, but the occupant will be exposed and at once surrounded by British soldiers. I spoke of the risk: it will be considerable unless we keep our heads and unless the accident appears perfectly natural and in no way contrived.'

Margesson expanded to the startled officers on his plan, a far from easy one to act upon considering the strength and closeness of the Cossack guard and the Russian infantry bearers who held the palanquin. But his idea was simple and held the possibility of success: an officer was to go ahead with the advanced scouting party when the march was resumed, and he was to report a force of tribesmen ahead, an ambush across the track. Every evidence of urgency, not to say panic, was to be manifested. The bugles would at once sound off for action, Margesson himself would hasten toward the palanquin, and a company of British soldiers, falling behind, would close in on the Cossack riders to reinforce the Russian guard on the Grand Duchess. In so doing, they would jostle both cavalry and palanquin-bearers – in short, create such havoc as they could, taking care to eject the palanquin's occupant. The York and Lancaster Regiment, as the flank battalion, would provide the scouting officer, whilst the 114th Highlanders, from their position ahead of the palanquin, would provide the upheaval company.

'You spoke of risk,' Dornoch pointed out. 'I see some considerable risk, General, if the Cossacks should open fire.'

'On us? I think not, Colonel, since they are very heavily outnumbered and in any case will have a common enemy to repel – for all they know! There may be blows, and you will warn your men to expect them and to take them philosophically–'

'Scots, sir, to take blows philosophically?'

'You must cool their Highland blood, Colonel. I don't propose to alter the relative positions in the column in case Count Tomislav should smell a rat in retrospect. What we shall have to hope for is that I shall be able to settle the issue peaceably. That is all, gentlemen. Kindly make your various dispositions. Brigade Major?'

Black saluted smartly. 'Sir?'

'My compliments to Count Tomislav. I would be honoured if he would take breakfast with me.' The Brigadier-General smiled coldly. 'Frugal he may find it – but it may give him food for thought!'

★   ★   ★

'Porridge, Count Tomislav?'

The Russian pursed his lips and made a sound of horror. 'A sticky substance, not wholesome. Thank you, but no.'

Margesson looked up at the hovering bearer. 'No porridge for the Count. Kedgeree – liver and bacon – fried eggs?'

'Kedgeree.'

Margesson nodded at the bearer. 'For me too. Also porridge. Coffee?'

The Russian smiled, showing his bad teeth, reached into a recess of his flowing garments and produced a silver flask which he thumped down on the trestle table between himself and the Brigadier-General. 'No coffee. Vodka. For you also?'

'Thank you – no.' Margesson put his head back a little and gave a loud sniff. He liked his drink as much as any man, but not at breakfast and a crack-of-dawn one at that. An early morning mouthful of whisky on a Scottish grouse moor was one thing, vodka with toast and marmalade quite another. He felt very slightly put off his diplomatic stroke by the sardonic look on Count Tomislav's hawk-like face, a look that said quite plainly that the British were a poor lot, a race of milksops. Margesson cleared his throat and gazed along the mountain peaks, splendid in their early-morning colourings of blue and purple, red and green and soft pink. Time was getting on: they must march soon, or fall behind on their route target. Porridge came for Margesson, kedgeree for the Russian. Margesson made a tentative probe during the porridge.

'The Grand Duchess, Count. I trust Her Imperial Highness is comfortable?'

'Yes.'

'There is nothing she requires?'

'Nothing.'

'I am at her service, of course.'

'Yes.'

There was a silence: kedgeree disappeared, and Count Tomislav gestured rather rudely towards his empty plate. Margesson, taking the hint, gestured in his turn at his bearer. 'More kedgeree for the Count.'

'Yes, Sahib.' The plate was removed, returned filled. Tomislav resumed eating. Margesson shifted about irritably on his camp stool, listening to the sounds from along the pass as the column made ready for the march: the rattle of rifles and equipment, the chink of harness and the creak of wagon-wheels from the commissariat, the Supply and Transport detachment. All along the line men were shaving in mirrors propped on cleft sticks, stripped to the waist for their ablutions but still with their rifles handy. Margesson glowered. A strong force of men at his disposal, and he was being stone-walled by a damn Russian – it was maddening considering what might be at stake: the fellow did nothing but eat!

Margesson tried again. 'I commanded a Guards battalion in London,' he said.

'Ah.'

'Palace duties largely.'

'Of course.'

'I met Her Majesty frequently – Queen Victoria.'

'An honour for you. Kedgeree is good. There is more, please?'

Margesson lifted his eyebrows at the patient bearer, who brought more kedgeree. Margesson said, 'There is another honour I have not yet had and would much appreciate.'

'Yes?'

'The honour of being presented to the Grand Duchess.'

'Yes.'

Margesson breathed hard, began to look glassy-eyed. 'I would be failing in my duty if I didn't request an audience, Count Tomislav. I have met her grandmother. Her

Majesty would expect no less than that I should wait upon her granddaughter. I have been excessively patient.'

Count Tomislav smiled, pushed away his plate without asking for more, and took a long pull at the flask of vodka. Wiping the back of his hand across wet lips when he had drunk, he smiled again and said, 'Her Britannic Majesty has the reputation of expecting very many things, General, some of them impossible. Already I have asked the Grand Duchess if she wishes to meet you, and she does not.'

Margesson spoke stiffly. 'I find that impossible to believe, Count Tomislav.'

'You accuse me of lying?'

'Oh, by no means, of course I don't! But ... don't you see ... a familiar face, someone from London and the Court–'

'Ah, but that is the point, General! The Grand Duchess is what you call, I think, sick of home–'

'Homesick.'

'Homesick, yes. This, she wishes not to make worse – as perhaps the sight of you would do. I do not wish to offend, nor does the Grand Duchess. But she does not wish to look at you. That is final.' Tomislav glanced up. 'There is more to eat?'

'Toast and marmalade,' Margesson said snappishly.

'Then toast and marmalade.'

'All he did was guzzle kedgeree,' the Brigadier-General reported angrily to his colonels. 'Never seen anything like it in all my life! Feller's a boor. Moreover, I didn't believe a word and I'm more anxious than ever, frankly, so the plan goes ahead.' He wagged his finger at Lord Dornoch. 'It's to be the sheerest accident, be sure of that, Colonel! The Cossacks must suspect nothing. I shall want a dependable officer in charge – I'll talk to him myself if you've no objection?' he added formally.

'None, sir, of course. I'll detail Captain Ogilvie's company – they'll change position in the column and march immediately ahead of the Russian guard–'

'Won't that arouse suspicions?'

Dornoch shook his head. 'I think not. In any case it's an acceptable risk in my opinion. Ogilvie's my most dependable company commander.'

'Yes ... they won't even notice a mere company changing ground, perhaps. Very well, Colonel, make your arrangements, if you please, and send Ogilvie to me.'

Margesson turned away with the Chief of Staff. Dornoch sent a runner for James Ogilvie. From Brigade another runner was despatched to the lines of the York and Lancaster Regiment who would provide the scouting party and the fake report of an ambush. When Ogilvie came up, Dornoch gave him a preliminary briefing before he reported to the Brigadier-General. Within half an hour the long column was fallen in to resume the march, with B Company of the Royal Strathspeys in rear of the lead battalion. Ahead, Margesson turned on his horse and lifted a hand: the orders were passed down the column by the battalion commanders to be repeated by the company commanders and the colour-sergeants with their broad crimson sashes standing out vividly in the sunlight on their khaki-drill tunics. The pipes and drums beat into life, a swelling note of war, and as the boots began crashing into the ground the clouds of dust rose around the marching knees, hanging in the still air so that it seemed as though the brigade were advancing through a low-lying morning mist hemmed in by the climbing hills around the track. The report from the scouts was to come one hour precisely from the time the column had started the march: James Ogilvie, having instructed his company in their forthcoming task, waited in a certain amount of trepidation. His part, he felt, was going to be trickier by far than the conduct of any mere patrol skirmish with the Pathan: it was not every day that a captain of infantry shot a granddaughter of Her Majesty from a palanquin, not every day that a regimental officer challenged the undoubted might of the Czar of All the Russias. Any slip was clearly going to have the widest possible repercussions, and the officer commanding the tumbling-out company would be very handily placed for the rose of scapegoat afterwards.

'Sir – the report as ordered, I fancy!'

It was the Chief of Staff who had spoken: in response the Brigadier-General raised his field-glasses and stared at the figure on horseback, galloping dangerously toward him along the pass. Margesson lost no time. Turning, he snapped, 'Enemy ambush ahead. Bugler!'

'Sir?'

'Sound the Alarm, then the Halt. Where's the Brigade Major?'

Black urged his horse towards the Brigadier-General and saluted. 'Here, sir.'

'Ride down the column, Brigade Major. Company commanders to get their men off the track and into cover.' Margesson gave a throaty chuckle. 'Every *assistance* is to be given the Russians and the palanquin's guard is to be reinforced as strongly as necessary.'

'Yes, sir.'

'Off you go, then! I shall ride toward the Grand Duchess shortly.'

'Yes, sir.' Saluting again, Black brought his horse round on its haunches and galloped back along the column. He noted, as he rode, a certain degree of confusion: the juxtaposition of the two bugle calls, echoing stridently off the rocky walls of the pass as the sound of the pipes and drums died away, had had an indecisive sound. The Alarm, and then the Halt, then nothing more until he, Andrew Black, could pass the verbal orders. Confusion was possibly what the Brigadier-General wished to cause in the circumstances, and if so he was succeeding. As Black rode shouting down the column the men were fallen out to vanish behind rocks and crevices, whilst in the rear of the Royal Strathspeys Ogilvie obeyed his particular orders.

Standing in his stirrups he called, 'B Company to remain in formation. Fall back and take up close escort on the Grand Duchess – at the double!' He turned his horse and rode down towards the Cossack guard, with Colour-Sergeant MacTrease running behind him and yelling the men on to follow and spread out along the flanks. Well versed by now in what they had to achieve, the Scots went in with a will, thrusting through the Russian horsemen, dodging hooves, causing surprise and consternation and indecision. Count Tomislav his face devilish, rode back through his own ranks, pushing his men aside, and reached out to Ogilvie, grasping his shoulder and almost pulling him from his horse.

'What are you trying to do?' he stormed.

'To reinforce the guard, sir.'

'It is not necessary–'

'I am ordered to do so.' Ogilvie rode forward.

'The devil take your orders, Captain! I am ordering you to go away and take your men with you. The Grand Duchess is a Russian responsibility!'

'And a British one also, Count Tomislav. If she should be taken by the Pathans–'

'She will not be. My sabre answers to that!

Let us hope, Captain, that it will not also have to answer for your life.' The Russian lifted his drawn sabre and held the blade across Ogilvie's throat. 'You will leave my ranks, Captain, or I shall slice off your head and have it served to your General to reinforce his luncheon table. Heed my words. I am not a man who says what he does not mean.'

They held each other's gaze: Ogilvie, reading the Russian's cold eyes and hard face, realised that indeed no idle threat had been uttered. He was, literally, within an inch of death. Looking sideways, he saw that two files of men under a lance-corporal were approaching the palanquin and starting to jostle the bearers. The manoeuvre was becoming less and less an accident, and more and more an intent by a controlled body of soldiers to take over the escort from the Cossacks – and such was not the Brigadier-General's plan at all. Ogilvie was now faced with a split-second decision: the moment the Scots moved near the palanquin, his head would roll at Count Tomislav's feet. The act would start a very present bloodbath in which his battalion would suffer and which would echo round the world in consequence. Ogilvie was about to climb down, to utter soothing words, when he heard his name shouted.

'Captain Ogilvie, sir! *Captain Ogilvie!*'

It was Cunningham, running dangerously for a man of his years and bulk, Cunningham red in the face and urgent. Ogilvie turned his face from the sabre's shining blade. 'Yes, Sar'nt-Major, what is it?'

'From the Colonel, sir – and from Brigade. The column's to advance and engage the enemy–'

'Engage, Sar'nt-Major?'

'Yes, sir! And you, Count Tomislav, sir.' Cunningham swung round towards the Russian. 'The tribe are mustered in force, and the Brigadier-General wishes you to hold the palanquin safe out of harm's way, sir, remaining in rear of the advance.'

The Russian nodded, glanced keenly at Ogilvie, and lowered his sabre. Ogilvie asked, 'And us, Sar'nt-Major?'

'To advance with the rest, sir, and leave the Grand Duchess to her Cossacks. I repeat, Captain Ogilvie, the tribes are out in strength, the biggest muster seen on the Frontier yet according to the scouts.' There was an unspoken message in Cunningham's eyes, and it was not hard to read: this had been no last minute reprieve from Brigade.

In a sense Margesson had been hoist with his own petard: the column was about to come under actual attack. A moment after the Regimental Sergeant-Major had finished speaking, the bugles rang out savagely along the pass, beating off the hillsides in confirmation that the brigade was to re-form and advance to action.

Chapter 5

Again Black was riding hard down the column, shouting. 'All company commanders to report at once to the General – at once, I say!'

With the rest, Ogilvie closed Brigade, his horse's hooves stumbling over rock, striking sparks, giving him a rough ride. Margesson looked eager for action: the Grand Duchess could wait now there was an enemy to beat off! In a strong voice the Brigadier-General summed up the position. 'Captain Haines of the York and Lancasters is the sole survivor of the scouting party. His men were attacked from behind – a case of *thuggee,* of strangulation silently done. Haines estimates the Pathans to number between fifteen hundred and two thousand, with artillery. They're across the pass around a bend four miles ahead.' He paused, looking at the faces of his officers, faces anticipatory but sombre: this was indeed a full muster.

Margesson went on confidently. 'We shall come through, gentlemen, I have no doubt of that. But it's going to be a hard fight, and our casualties will be heavy. Does anybody say that in the special circumstances we should retreat?'

There was no answer. Ogilvie, studying the faces, found a mixture of emotions. Andrew Black was swallowing hard, his eyes holding a feverish look: Black had always had a regard for his own skin, though once in action he responded well enough. Lord Dornoch's face was grave: he would perhaps never make a general for he could never be ruthless when it came to casualties in the regiment. He looked upon the 114th as a family with himself the father; and ahead there clearly lay much blood that day. For different reasons both he and Black would like to urge retreat; but neither spoke.

Margesson spoke for them. 'I dislike unnecessary bloodshed as much as any man. Retreat is possible in a physical sense – we are only an escort when all is said and done, and I have no particular wish to assist Russian schemes whatever the Viceroy may have decided. But we represent the Raj, and so I shall not retreat. If a British brigade should show unwillingness to fight an enemy of half its strength, the result might be disastrous for the Raj. Lord Dornoch?'

'Sir?'

'The Pathans know we're coming. We'll march proudly. My compliments to your Pipe-Major. His most stirring tune to put the fear of God into the heathen!'

Margesson nodded a dismissal: the officers rode back briskly to their own battalions and companies, and the orders were passed to the subalterns and colour-sergeants. In the van Pipe-Major Ross, striding ahead with his kilt swinging about his knees, puffed air into his pipes. As the drums began to beat, the Highland music came out strongly, all the pipers blowing from full chests till *Farewell to Invermore* seemed to fill the very pass to bring alive the home-thoughts of distant Scotland and the hills and glens of Speyside. Down the column, scowling his dislike of Scots music which ranked in his mind with Scots oatmeal, Count Tomislav brought his supply train into the close escort's umbrella – the mule-carts and the covered wagons, one of which contained, uncomfortably, the attendant ladies of the court. His mountain gun-battery he brought up on the flanks, close by the lurching palanquin, the barrels still strapped to the sides of the ambling mules: they could be assembled almost within seconds when the need should arise to bring them into action. The march continued, the pace not being forced: in Margesson's own time now, they would engage the enemy. There was excited and fearful chatter from the women's wagon, chatter which made Count Tomislav scowl the more as he heard it: ladies of the court or not, he sent an officer to bid them shut their pretty mouths. More chatter came from the camp-followers straggling behind, that inevitable impediment to any army in the field in India, containing as it did the filthy Untouchables who performed the army's low-grade housework, its menial chores and tasks unfitted to white men, to conquerors. Their chatter Count Tomislav bore angrily but with fortitude: they were a British responsibility, a more tiresome one than his own obedient Russian peasants, and the British could get on with it. He had his own responsibilities to his Czar, and they were onerous ones.

As the head of the column neared the bend in the pass, Margesson's field-glasses picked out the signs of life: snaky bayonets glinting in the sun, turbaned heads, hairy faces, tattered garments – the Pathan scouts along the heights, reporting back the British advance to the army waiting in its ambush below.

'We can't use the guns till we turn the corner,' Margesson said. 'It'll be up to the infantry to take the first of the brunt. They can go in behind their bayonets, and I'll use the guns as soon as they can bear on a clear target. How's that damned Russian?'

'As ready for action as we are, sir,' the Chief of Staff answered. 'I think we can leave the Grand Duchess to his care without too much anxiety.'

Margesson grunted. 'I hope so indeed! We must remember she's the whole reason why we're here at all.'

'Sir?'

'I mean, in the last resort, she's the one we make a stand for.' Margesson lifted his glasses again. 'I wish I could see round bloody corners, Maurice! Till I know the enemy's present dispositions, I can't give precise orders for attack. Do we assume them to have gone into cover up the hill-sides ... or will they still be solid across the track? Do we charge, or do we scatter?'

Colonel Maurice shrugged. 'It's one of the imponderables. I'd settle for some of both.

They know we know they're there, so there's no point in them trying to hide their whole force.'

Margesson said no more, riding on in silence, approaching victory or defeat, hand teasing his clipped moustache. Despite earlier words of confidence, despite his keen manner, he was in fact full of private doubts. He had not served before in India, had never before commanded in the field: during his time with the Grenadier Guards his regiment had not been in any action and his experience had been confined to those palace duties of which he had spoken to Count Tomislav, and to very infrequent exercises in and around such outlandish places as Aldershot, Colchester and the Curragh – in the Irish camp, some of the natives had indeed been as wild as the Pathans, but by no means as hostile. Margesson felt a distinct looseness in his bowels, accompanied by a sense of shame and mortification that a Brigadier-General should be subject to such a feeling. It was not – most certainly it was not – that he feared shot or shell. His fear was that he would give the wrong order, make the wrong appraisal of the situation that would so soon confront him. He had already taken experienced advice, for he was not such a fool as to let pride blind him; but his alone must be the actual decision and it must be made in a split-second as he came with the head of the brigade round the turn in the pass, and saw what was to be seen. A wrong word then, and many deaths would ensue: Margesson came out in a cold sweat at the thought of a débâcle. In defeat he would be spoken of with derision in the regimental messes of the Empire, if his name were to be mentioned at all. His clubs would be closed to him, ladies would put up their fans at his approach, and turn away. London would be a nightmare, the very policemen's eyes accusing him in the streets of worse than murder. Generals were always news, and successful ones were public idols, their faces well known to all men. But bad news travelled much faster than good...

Brigadier-General Margesson straightened his back and scowled ahead towards the now clearly visible cleft in the hills that indicated the bend. His manner was cool now, his face more relaxed when the scowl departed. He had remembered some advice given him when first he had arrived in Peshawar – advice tendered by no less than a person than Lieutenant-General Francis

Fettleworth, commander of the First Division: 'When in doubt, when worried, as you will be upon occasion,' Bloody Francis had said, taking his arm in a hard and almost emotional grip, 'think of Her Majesty the Queen. It helps enormously, very *steadying* – you'll see!'

It worked as promised. That regal little shape, for all the world like a somewhat bosomy pear, the white bun of hair beneath the widow's cap contrasting strongly with the funeral but majestic black of the rest of it, lofted out its compelling will and presence over the far-flung Indian pass. And Brigadier-General Margesson responded to it fittingly as from ahead the fresh scouts, not so far advanced now, came running back with word for Brigade.

'Sir, the enemy are across the pass and up the hillsides, in full view.'

Margesson nodded. 'You were right, Maurice,' he remarked to the Chief of Staff. 'Brigade Major?'

'Sir?'

'The moment we ride into view of the enemy, the bugles will sound the General Advance, and the Brigade will charge the enemy in column with bayonets fixed. Kindly inform my colonels at once.'

'Yes, sir—'

'And tell Major Barrington he is to be ready to assemble his battery and go into action at the same time but will hold his fire until I order him to open.'

'Sir!' Saluting, Black brought his horse round and went off at the gallop. Ten minutes later Margesson at the head of the column rounded the bend in the pass. As he lifted his hand the bugles sounded out, strident and commanding. The Brigadier-General and his personal staff rode forward at the gallop, with the regiments doubling up behind them, cheering and shouting with the sun striking brilliant fire from the massed bayonets, fanning out on the flanks so far as possible in the confines of the hills. As the bugles blew, the horde of wild Pathans opened fire from ahead. Colonel Maurice, Chief of Staff, fell headlong from his horse with blood pouring from his neck. As his horse dashed on riderless, the pounding feet of the lead battalion smashed over his body. Everywhere men were falling, screaming out in agony; the fire had become an enfilading one, and was intense, the bullets thudding into the running bodies, unable to miss the tight-packed target of the long column. But there was no check in the advance: the Royal Strathspeys charged on, yelling Highland oaths, outrunning the Brigadier-General whose horse had been shot from under him. Margesson was stumbling over the rocky track, clasping his left arm. Helmetless, he was shouting encouragement to his men. Ogilvie, riding ahead fast, pulled his own horse aside just in time to avoid running him down, and, sliding from the saddle, went to Margesson's aid.

'Sir, your arm–'

'Collar-bone broken. You're Ogilvie, aren't you?'

'Yes, sir–'

'Carry on, Ogilvie, don't worry about me. Just a moment though. I'll take your horse if you don't mind. Give me a leg up, young feller.'

Ogilvie did as ordered. Puffing a little, Margesson made the saddle and thrust his booted feet into the stirrups. Without further word he rode ahead, straight for the enemy, clutching the reins with his right hand and leaving his left arm to dangle and sway agonisingly as he rode. Ogilvie, with his revolver in his hand, plunged after the Brigadier-General on foot, dodging the whining Pathan bullets miraculously, feeling their brief wind across his face, feeling one zip into his Wolseley helmet to send it spinning towards the flank. A moment later he heard the mountain battery thundering into action from beside the track, smelt the sharp tang of gunsmoke and saw the flashes twinkling like fireworks along the bottom of the hillside. Shells crashed down on to the Pathan hordes, pitting the ranks with flame to leave sudden gaps that were as quickly filled with more yelling tribesmen. Then the Pathan artillery opened up from its precarious positions on rock ledges in the hillsides, sending its projectiles down on the British ranks. Ogilvie, looked around quickly, saw that Barrington was unable to elevate his guns sufficiently to bring them to bear on the native crews. Catching sight of Colour-Sergeant MacTrease, Ogilvie shouted to him.

'Sir?'

'B Company to fall out of the general advance, Colour-Sar'nt–'

'*Fall out*, Captain Ogilvie, sir?'

Ogilvie nodded breathlessly. 'Yes, fall out and take cover – snipe at the gun crews. See to it, Colour-Sar'nt!'

'Sir!' MacTrease turned about, looking this way and that, began yelling at B Company as the men ran past firing. He shouted them down into cover, rough cover behind rocky outcrops and such scrubby bushes as they could find. Men flung themselves flat, took aim at the blazing guns, and fired. In the rear of the column the men of the Border Regiment, led by their Colonel on the one side and by their Regimental Sergeant-Major on the other, were doing their best to clear the Pathans from their superior positions on the twin hillsides, concentrating their fire there and leaving the other two battalions to engage the solid mass holding the track itself. They appeared, Ogilvie noticed, to be having a measure of success: one after another the tribesmen were flinging up their arms and falling spread-eagled, crashing down onto the jagged rocks along the track, while the British rifles ahead were cutting down the enemy as they tried to replace the flank casualties. The enfilading fire was growing less. As for the palanquin containing the Grand Duchess, this was stationary; laid upon the ground, it was covered with heavily filled sacks from the Russians' commissariat – sacks, apparently, of four and rice and other eatables, into which bullets were thudding to spill out the contents. The Cossack guard was bunched about the palanquin, facing outwards and firing continuously, in something approaching British square formation. Count Tomislav, his eyes blazing, was striding up and down waving his sabre and shouting in his own language, seeming untouched by the whining bullets and the artillery bursts. Ogilvie, from his position with B Company, was firing whenever he found a target within revolver range: his shooting was good. He winged one man about to plunge a long-handled knife into the unprotected back of the Regimental Sergeant-Major, who was engaged in hand-to-hand combat with a huge sinewy native dressed only in a loin-cloth. Cunningham fought on unheeding, was joined by a lance-corporal who smashed in the native's head with a savagely wielded rifle-butt. Blood and brain spattered over Cunningham, who stood back with his chest heaving and his face scarlet with his exertions. Breath regained, the R.S.M. dashed ahead to join the main body of the battalion. Then there came one of those curious lulls in the racket of the battle that Ogilvie had often noted during previous Frontier engagements: a brief space during which all present on both sides seemed almost by mutual consent to cease firing, to take stock and to take breath together before plunging back into death and destruction. And into that momentary pause of war came the loud and stirring wail of the Royal Strathspeys' pipers, playing *"Cock o' the North"*, the regimental tune of war and attack. It acted like magic on the Scots: Ogilvie saw Lord Dornoch leap up on a jag of rock and wave his revolver above his head. He heard the Colonel's shout, carrying down the pass:

'*Craig Elachaidh ... Stand fast, Craigellachie!*'

The traditional war-cry was taken up, as the lull lasted, right down the line of the Royal Strathspeys. As the firing started up once more, ending the quiet, a roar came from all the Scots' throats and the 114th surged forward as one, renewing the charge on a wave of fighting fervour that carried them right into the mass of Pathans, firing, thrusting with blood-red bayonets, trampling, swinging rifle-butts as the magazines emptied, smashing heads and shoulders. The impact of the tremendous infantry charge, the sheer fighting lust of the Highlanders, swayed the native horde. They began to fight towards their rear, trampling down their own kind, and those already on the far side streamed away with a somewhat unusual haste to quit the fight, down along the pass or fast up the hillsides where they were picked off by a sustained and murderous fire from the flank battalion of the York and Lancasters, assisted by the sharpshooters of the Border Regiment. Thanks to the efforts of B Company of the 114th, the native guns were by now largely silent, though casualties were still being caused by those remaining in action.

Margesson, his left arm forced tightly in against his side, stood in his stirrups. 'Reform!' he shouted. 'One more effort, men, and we'll have 'em on the run!' He gestured to his attendant bugler, and a call rang out, loud and challenging along the rocky pass. The whole column surged towards the Pathan mob once again, passing right through to form up on the track beyond, leaving the native force at the mercy now of Barrington's mountain battery. Shouting the orders to depress and open, Barrington's was the final say: a rain of explosive thundered into the native levies, splitting the very ground from under them, shattering bodies, filling the air with flying splinters of rock and steel. This completed the rout: the company of Scots ran in pursuit of the fleeing Pathans until they were recalled by the bugles sounding Retire. Margesson, in spite of his painful arm and shoulder, was smiling in happy triumph until, looking all about him, he took in the numbers of casualties. Already the medical details were busy with bandages and ointments and the stretcher-parties were carrying the most severely wounded men to the makeshift field dressing station set up jointly by Surgeon-Major Corton and the Medical Officers of the two English battalions. There was much obvious pain, and much stoicism.

'A count of the dead, Brigade Major,' Margesson said solemnly, his own face twisted with pain. 'A nominal roll, if you please – and burial parties to be detailed at once.'

'Yes, sir.'

'And I want to know about the wounded. See to it that the Pathan wounded are also attended to.'

'The Pathans, sir – *the natives*?' Black sounded scandalised.

'If you please, Brigade Major,' Margesson said coldly, then saw Lord Dornoch riding up, weary and blood-stained, with a linen handkerchief roughly tied about his forehead. 'Dornoch, you're wounded?'

'Oh, a trifle, nothing more – a bullet skimmed away some flesh.' Dornoch ran a critical eye over Margesson's bloodied shoulder and arm. 'You're in a much worse state, sir. Let me call up the medicos.'

Margesson brushed the suggestion aside. 'No, no, there are men close to dying – I shall live!' He changed the subject brusquely. 'Colonel, your men did splendidly. I congratulate them through you for now – I shall speak to them personally later on. A splendid charge!'

'Thank you, sir. The Pathans never did like our Highland bayonets.'

'So it would appear.' Margesson glanced after Andrew Black, who was riding off on his various errands. 'That feller Black. What's your policy in regard to the native wounded, Dornoch?'

Dornoch raised his eyebrows. 'My policy, General?'

'Do your medicos treat 'me or don't they?'

Dornoch said, 'Indeed they do, just as they treat our own wounded. Why d'you ask, sir?'

'Because Black seems to think they should *not* be treated.'

There was a short laugh from Lord Dornoch. 'I know! Black believes dark skin feels no pain. It's not an uncommon belief out here, more especially amongst the rank and file, General.'

'Then they should be taught differently, including your Captain Black! A few homilies, I think, would not come amiss after we return to cantonments, Colonel.'

'As you say, sir.'

Margesson stared with a touch of belligerence. 'You sound indifferent.'

'Not indifferent, General. A mere question of priorities. Even I put our own men first if there are shortages of medical supplies – as usually there are!'

Slowly, Margesson nodded. 'Point noted! Oh, I'm no do-gooder, Dornoch, nor a Pathan lover either. Perhaps I'm not so inured to Frontier service as you – that's all!' He winced, clearly in a great deal of pain. 'How's that bloody palanquin, d'you know?'

'I'm afraid I've had other things to do,' Dornoch said mildly.

'H'm. Well, we're lucky – it doesn't seem to have been a prime target for the Pathans' fire.'

'I'd be much surprised if it were,' Dornoch said with a laugh.

'Why's that?'

'No point in capturing a dead Grand

Duchess, is there?'

'Good gracious!' Margesson seemed quite startled as the implication struck him. 'Are you saying, in effect, that you think that attack was premeditated, carried out as a result of some positive knowledge?'

'Indeed I am, sir.'

'But the fullest secrecy's been maintained!'

'Has it?' Dornoch laughed again. 'My dear sir, there's no secrecy along the North-West Frontier, as you must surely have suspected. We knew, Division knew, Army Command in Murree knew ... not to mention Ootacamund and Calcutta – and Katmandu. The bush telegraph will have seen to the rest!'

'But what would a bunch of damn natives want with the Grand Duchess, Dornoch?'

Dornoch gave him a shrewd, amused look. 'A bargaining counter, don't you think – and a good one, the very best?'

Margesson blew out his cheeks. 'By jingo! Her Majesty's granddaughter, to become a pawn of Frontier politics! Why, it's unthinkable!'

'But wholly possible.'

'Have they the intelligence ... the sort of general savvy and background to make use of a royal personage, Dornoch? Aren't they just a bunch of savages – highwaymen, if you like, thugs, tribesmen in smelly clothes, just out to fight anybody who happens to come along, just for the immediate pickings? Isn't that a fair appreciation?'

'Nine times out of ten, yes. I have a feeling we've struck the tenth, sir. And as I said – not by accident but by design.'

Margesson scowled along the pass, still heavy with the stench of fighting, of blood and gunsmoke. He felt uneasy. The Brigade of Guards could scarcely be blamed for his failure to penetrate the mind of the dirty native... 'I think,' he said suddenly, 'I'll have another word with that starving Cossack.' He swung round on his runner, 'My compliments to Count Tomislav. I'd be obliged if he'd attend Brigade immediately.'

Saluting, the runner doubled away. Occasional shots were heard, and the shatter of lead against rock: some of the natives were on the heights still, harassing the column. The rifles answered: Margesson watched as a tattered body lifted its arms and fell, bouncing off the sides to land with a head split open on a cruel, upward-pointing jag in the pass. Dornoch excused himself, saying he must attend upon his battalion and find out the casualties. An anxious man because of those casualties, he rode away from Brigade. He passed the General's runner, going back towards his master, his eyes staring. Within a couple of minutes Lord Dornoch heard his name being shouted with some urgency, and he returned wearily to Brigade.

Margesson was looking white, his eyes staring like those of his runner. He said, 'By jingo, Dornoch, there's real trouble now! The damn palanquin. It's gone. With Her Imperial Highness!'

Chapter 6

The gentleman in the sombre black morning coat, sitting bolt upright on the padded seat behind his coachman and clasping his hands over a heavy silver-handled walking-stick, looked thoughtful, no more, as he stared out at the spring-fresh fields of Brentford, Isleworth, Hounslow, heading westward for the peace and tranquillity of Datchet and his routine appointment at Windsor Castle. However, behind that merely thoughtful expression, Lord Salisbury was a prey to many anxieties. In many ways the 1890s were proving troublous years for a Conservative Prime Minister: the alliance with the Liberal Unionists was at times wearisome, and Lord Salisbury had had to bend to certain prevailing winds in matters domestic, though in education affairs the strong High Churchman that dwelt within him had seen to it that the Liberal Unionists toed that particular line.

Foreign policy, however, was Salisbury's real interest, and in the conduct of this he excelled and knew he excelled. Caution was his watchword: caution led to success. Success, in Lord Salisbury's book, lay in preserving the peace in Europe. In Eastern affairs his touch was perhaps less sure, and today, bowling along the high roads out of Westminster, he knew that Her Majesty intended to probe, with her usual cruel ability to seek out weak points, on matters pertaining to certain of her Prime Minister's policies in regard to the Indian Empire. Thus it was with a high degree of reluctance that Lord Salisbury finally breasted the hill to the castle gateway and, gravely lifting his tall hat to the bearskinned sentries' marks of respect, passed through the great arch and into the quadrangle to have his carriage door opened for him by a bowing flunkey in bewigged livery.

The Prime Minister stepped down, carrying his silk hat in his left hand. 'Good morning,' he said. 'Where's Her Majesty to be found, pray?'

'In the private apartments, my Lord.'

'I see.' Lord Salisbury turned and stumped across to the east side of the quadrangle. There was a small frown on his face now:

the use of the private apartments for his official call suggested some indisposition; when indisposed, Her Majesty tended to be less patient than usual. At such times only her dear Disraeli, dead these many years, could have handled her successfully. But no matter: Lord Salisbury steeled himself. Duty was duty! Escorted by more flunkeys headed now by one of the Queen's personal household, Lord Salisbury entered the private apartments, making his way to the Queen's drawing-room. At the far end, with a small dog crouched at the hem of her wide black skirt, the Queen-Empress sat gazing out of a window, elbow on the arm of her chair, the hand supporting her chin. Beyond the window, beyond the terrace, lay the splendid sunken garden, much loved by the old Queen.

Lord Salisbury approached, silently across the thick carpet, stared at by clusters of photographs, surrounded by ornaments and bric-a-brac. The Queen turned her head, inclined it graciously.

'Your Majesty.' The Prime Minister bowed, heels together.

'Dear Lord Salisbury! We are glad to see you, for we find the days long and lonely.'

'Indeed, Ma'am.'

'Pray sit down.'

'Thank you, Ma'am.' The Prime Minister sat on a brocaded chair with spindly walnut legs, close to the Queen, eyeing the small dog with caution as he did so. Her Majesty's pets were apt to be jealous, and spiteful too. 'I trust Your Majesty is not unwell?'

'A trifling indisposition,' the Queen answered off-handedly. 'We've been prescribed a powder which should make us well.' The autocratic face tightened up suddenly. 'What is the news from India, Prime Minister?'

'There has been nothing fresh, Ma'am, since–'

'How is our granddaughter?'

Salisbury brought out a handkerchief and blew his nose. 'I beg your pardon, Ma'am. Er ... the Princess Elizabeth ... again, there has been no word as yet – there's scarcely been the time, you–'

'We are anxious for her safety, Lord Salisbury, and hold you answerable for it, since it was your advice that we should not try to stop her journey.' A flush had now appeared on the Queen's face, and she had straightened her back against the cushions that supported her. 'One would not imagine such delays! There are such things as telegrams, are there not?'

'Certainly, Ma'am—'

'Then we consider Lord Elgin discourteous!' the Queen snapped.

Lord Salisbury sighed inwardly: the mood was difficult. Tactfully he said, 'Ma'am, the Princess Elizabeth is already started upon her journey inside India – we know that she passed Fort Jamrud safely. Whilst on the march, it is not possible to establish contact—'

'Fiddlesticks!'

'Ma'am—'

'We believe our Engineers are expert with the field telegraph.'

'A line has not been laid, Ma'am.'

'Why has it not?'

'A military unnecessity, Ma'am. Besides being impracticable ... the whole march to Katmandu is little short of a thousand miles.'

'Then runners! What are human feet, or horses, for?'

'Ma'am,' the Prime Minister said with restraint, 'your granddaughter is in the best possible hands. Brigadier-General Margesson, whom you know, will send a runner at once if ever he should see fit to do so – you may rest assured! Why, there is an entire infantry brigade with the Princess, and guns – and there is a Scots regiment, in addition to her own Cossack guard–'

'*Her* own Cossack guard!' the Queen broke in bitterly. '*Our* guard is her guard, my dear Lord Salisbury, since she is one of our closest family, and you have *no* need to say what you were about to, for we shall say it for you: the Princess Elizabeth is married now and none of our concern. To that we say, as we said just now *fiddlesticks!*'

Lord Salisbury inclined his head. 'Yes, Ma'am.' He said no more: there was nothing pertinent to say, thus to say anything must appear an impertinence. He must wait, and he waited: the Queen, her bosom heaving, turned a stony face towards the window. From beside an impatiently tapping black-shod foot, the small dog stared with bright eyes at the Prime Minister, teeth slightly bared. Lord Salisbury, meeting its baleful look, felt that Ma'am had by some alchemy of her will transferred her anger to the dog. Once again, Lord Salisbury blew his nose and then continued waiting, fixing his attention meanwhile on the crowding photographs of Her Majesty's family in their heavy silver frames: His Royal Highness the Prince of Wales, large and rumbustious in his uniform as Admiral of the fleet, with his son the Duke of York, small and punctilious as a naval captain; the Princess Victoria, Princess Royal of England, married to one German Emperor, mother of another; Prince Alice, married to the Grand Duke of Hesse; Prince Alfred, Duke of Edinburgh and Grand Duke of Saxe-Coburg and Gotha; Princess Helena Augusta, now a princess of Schleswig-Holstein; Princess Louise, Duchess of Argyll; and sundry others, an exhaustive line completed by veritable classrooms-full of grandchildren of various ages including the Princess Elizabeth Fedorovna herself. But the image most often to be found staring Lord Salisbury in the eye was that of the late Prince Albert, the Queen's beloved Consort... At length the Queen relaxed and turned her face to her Prime Minister. 'What do the Russians want?' she demanded. 'We have had no sense out of Czar Nicholas for some time, nor you either, my dear Lord Salisbury!'

'Ma'am, with the very greatest respect, I have already told you–'

'Then tell us again!' the Queen said peremptorily. 'When you were last in attendance, you spoke at great length about the

European Conference in 1875, about the likelihood of war with Russia two years later when you succeeded our dear Lord Derby at the Foreign Office ... and about how you arranged an Anglo-Russian agreement with Schouvalov before the conference in Berlin.'

A fan was tapped against the arm of the chair. 'Pray come to more modern times now.'

'Yes, Ma'am. On that latter occasion – at Berlin – I achieved peace with honour, if you remember–'

'Yes, yes!'

'But since then the Court at St Petersburg has developed fresh ambitions in regard to our North-West Frontier provinces.'

'But Nepal, Lord Salisbury?'

'Ah, Nepal is a new threat – or a new *possible* threat, Ma'am. If the Czar can secure concessions from the King...' Lord Salisbury hesitated: in Nepal, the real power happened to reside in the Prime Minister, not the King, as it was his duty to point out in order fully to inform Her Majesty; but, in someone who was also a Prime Minister, and addressing his monarch, such precision might well be deemed an impertinence. Discretion was called for. 'If the Czar can secure concessions from the government of

Nepal, Ma'am, then British India will have a dangerous enemy poised upon its northern borders.

'Yes. But why send our granddaughter?'

Salisbury pursed his lips. 'Diplomacy, Ma'am, diplomacy! The ways of both the Russian and of the diplomat are always clouded in mystery, yet I believe this one to be penetrable nevertheless.' He leaned forward. 'As I explained at our previous audience–'

'We know what you explained. That Nepal is friendly towards us, that we have a Resident in Katmandu, and that the presence of a British princess as emissary of St Petersburg might ... what was it you said, Lord Salisbury?'

'That Her Royal Highness's presence might be contrived by the Czar to indicate the blessing of Whitehall upon his desires, Ma'am.'

The bosom heaved. 'Such – such *chicanery!*'

'Indeed, Ma'am, and of course deplorable–'

'And that is why I ask, why send our granddaughter?'

'It is the Czar who sent–'

'Fiddlesticks!' the Queen said for the third

time. '*We* gave our assent, and that made her journey possible. In our opinion, *we* sent her. Why?'

'Ma'am, you did agree–'

'I know!' The Queen's foot began tapping again, angrily. 'We may perhaps change our mind, since we have now thought a great deal more about this. Will you please tell us *why* our granddaughter is in such terribly dangerous country upon a mission that in its whole concept is inimical to the Raj?' The Queen's eyes seemed to bore into the Prime Minister like red-hot irons. 'Last time we believe you put us off with idle nonsense, with *fibs*–'

'Fibs?' Salisbury was shaken.

'Lies, then. Kindly don't answer back. You spoke about the undesirability of angering the Russian Court by interference – a *rude* word of itself. To do that, you insisted, would be to invite some more *underhand* Russian approach to the King of Nepal – did you not?'

'I did, Ma'am. Some other approach might have been harder to combat.'

'But that was not the whole truth, Lord Salisbury.'

'Upon my honour, Ma'am, it was.'

In silence, the Queen stared at him. From

113

above the fireplace a French clock struck the hour, and outside a military band began playing "The British Grenadiers": Her Majesty's foot tapped differently now, not in anger but in time to the beat of her First Regiment of Foot Guards, and a rapt expression stole over the round, imperious face. The brass marched away out of earshot, and the Queen turned her attention back to her Prime Minister. She said, 'We respect your honour, dear Lord Salisbury, but now you must tell us what lies behind the truth. We do not flatter ourselves that our ministers tell us *everything* till they are *forced* to do so. We are, after all, a woman of the world.'

Salisbury shook his head, sighed, took a deep breath. 'You have had the truth, Ma'am.' Bracing himself against yet another fiddlesticks which in fact did not come, he went on, 'There is perhaps one thing that underlies the truth, and it is this: the presence of the Princess Elizabeth is enabling us to put our army into Nepal with an excellent excuse for being there—'

'That,' the Queen said complacently. 'is *exactly* what we arrived at after our further consideration, and it leads to another question: why did Czar Nicholas, who must know all this, request a British escort?'

'Why, Ma'am, because he knew he wouldn't be given passage at all without it!'

'Then why cross our territory at all? There are other ways, are there not?'

'Yes, through Tibet. We have made enquiries. Tibet refused passage to the Czar, Ma'am.'

'I see,' the Queen said shortly. She stared at Salisbury: Salisbury was uncomfortably aware of an old-fashioned quality in her face, a beheading look. 'We have already told you, we have the impression you were not entirely honest with us upon your last visit. This we deplore, and never mind what we said earlier about our knowing the ways of politicians. We also have the impression that our beloved granddaughter is about to be used as a pawn in a very dangerous business, and in a very dangerous country full of little men with *kukris*–'

'Ma'am, your Ghurka regiments–'

'Oh, our Ghurka regiments are brave and loyal, to be sure, but not all the Nepalese have enlisted!' The Queen lifted a walking-stick that so far had remained concealed in the fastnesses of her arm-chair. This she pointed at the Prime Minister, who had the feeling it represented in her mind the orb, the sceptre and the crown. 'Enough of it!' she said with asperity. 'We do not play games with the Czar and fall in line with his rules. We withdraw our consent. Our grand-daughter is to be taken to Peshawar or Nowshera, and–'

'Ma'am! The Czar–'

'We do not care a pin for the Czar, dear Lord Salisbury. You will do as we say and you will *not* argue. Lord Elgin is to be in-formed *at once*. Our granddaughter is still upon our own territory, I take it–'

'Yes, indeed she–'

'Then hurry back to Whitehall, Prime Minister.' The Queen reaching out, tugged mightily at the richly-embroidered bell-pull hanging beside the massive fireplace. Mustering such dignity as he could, Lord Salisbury rose to his feet as a footman enter-ed the drawing-room, bowed to the Queen, and backed away to the door. Entering his waiting carriage, his head was jostled by anxious thoughts for the ensuing diplomatic activity to be brought about by changes of royal minds; and also by the most disloyal ponderings on the interfering tactics of arrogant old ladies with too little to occupy their days...

Immediately upon the Prime Minister's

arrival back in Downing Street, a meeting of the Cabinet was called.

'Your Excellency!'

The figure in the immense four-poster bed stirred, the content of deep sleep suddenly broken into. An eye opened. 'What is it?' The Viceroy saw his A.D.C., immaculately uniformed and carrying a lighted lamp.

'Your Excellency, I have a most urgent telegram from London.'

'From whom, in London?'

'From the Secretary of State, sir, at the India Office, with the authority of Her Majesty.'

'Good God!' Lord Elgin sat up, glanced at his wife, who had not woken. 'Come, man, where is it?'

The A.D.C. held out the cable form and brought the lamp closer to the Viceroy. Elgin read, anger and astonishment showing clearly in his face. 'I'll be damned! I'm ordered to withdraw the Grand Duchess! How the devil do I when she's surrounded by her own Cossack guard?' He looked up at the A.D.C. 'Has the Military Secretary seen this?'

'Yes, sir. He's in attendance outside, in case—'

'What's his view?'

'He sees dangers, sir, and would like to disregard the order.'

'So would I,' Elgin said in a harsh voice. 'Ask the Military Secretary to come in.'

Late next day in Peshawar, the final decision of the Viceroy was paraphrased by a sergeant of the Duke of Cornwall's Light Infantry in cantonments: 'Orders, my lucky lads, is bloody orders and as such to be bloody well obeyed, so look smart. Clean bodies and clean rifles, and fall in 0530 sharp or you'll have me on your bloody backs from here to bloody Bodmin.' He looked critically around the half-company detailed to make contact with Margesson's brigade, thinking of the widening rings that spread when the royal word was dropped into the pool of Empire. For that incredible communicator, the bush telegraph, had already spread the information – albeit, no doubt, based upon guesswork – that the Queen-Empress herself had taken charge. So from royal Windsor Castle, via the Prime Minister in Cabinet, via the Secretary of State for India and the Viceroy in Council, via the Commander-in-Chief and the Northern Army Commander who, rumour said, had spun like a top, via the Lieutenant-General Commanding the First Division, via Brigade and via the Colonel of the Duke of Cornwall's and his Adjutant, and their own Company Commander ... right down the line the ripples had come, to end in orders for an extended march to God alone knew exactly where, on the part of – in the sergeant's eyes – the rawest lot of farm-hands ever to reach him from the regimental depot in the sleepy old town of Bodmin.

Chapter 7

The Brigadier-General was beside himself: no officer could hope to survive the loss of royalty. Riding with his staff down the column, still licking its wounds and counting its dead, his face held an almost lunatic glare. Coming upon men of the Border Regiment, seemingly no more than a remnant of a fine battalion, he raved for explanations: one was given by a swaying colour-sergeant whose face was a mask of blood.

'The Cossacks, sir. They turned and ran.'

'The devil they did! With the Grand Duchess?'

'Aye, sir.' The N.C.O.'s voice was weak but bitter. 'The bastards fought through our ranks, sir, using their sabres.'

'Good God! Where's your Colonel, man?'

'Dead, sir–'

'The Russians?'

'No, sir, a Pathan bullet. And the Major,

120

sir. There's not many of us left, sir. The Pathans cut off the rear...' The Colour-Sergeant staggered, reaching out for Margesson's horse in an attempt to steady himself. Black, dismounting fast, ran forward and caught the man as he lurched towards the ground. Laying him down on the dust-strewn track, he felt for the heart, then looked up at Margesson.

'He's gone, sir.'

Dully, Margesson nodded, staring back along the pass to the rear. Already to east and west the vultures were gathering to hover in their clouds of funeral black; one or two, unable to wait for their meal, dropped down to peck with ravening beaks at the bloody corpses, pulling and tearing until they were driven off, screeching, by the infuriated survivors to resume their tireless vigil above the jagged peaks. Margesson, taking a grip upon himself, turned in his saddle and called to Black.

'Brigade Major, my compliments to Colonel Gill of the York and Lancasters. He is to take three companies with all available horses to act as Mounted Infantry and ride back to the west. That palanquin can't have gone far. It is to be brought back.'

'Yes, sir.'

'And the guns will march in support – I expect no further attack from the Pathans. Inform Major Barrington.'

'Yes, sir. And the rest of the column, sir?'

'We remain here,' Margesson said, his chin jutting, 'to receive the palanquin – and Count Tomislav.'

Black saluted and turned to head up the column. With Lord Dornoch, the Brigadier-General waited. Quickly the York and Lancasters' detail was mounted from the 300-odd horses of the brigade complement, and formed up for the westward chase. As they came past, Margesson muttered, 'So many damn bags of hay, but they'll have to do.' Raising his voice he called out to Gill, 'They'll not be far. I'll give you one hour, then I shall assume you need assistance. If I hear gunfire, I'll make the assumption immediately. Good luck, Colonel.'

'Thank you, sir.' Colonel Gill saluted. His Mounted Infantry rode out in a rising cloud of dust, followed by the dismantled guns of the mountain battery strapped to the plodding mules. As they drew away westwards, Margesson's face was grim: Count Tomislav was about to be taught some of the duties of a soldier, the first being that, whatever his charge, he did not cut down British infantry in a headlong flight to the rear. If British soldiers were to die, they would die fighting the common enemy, not a supposedly friendly escort! The more he thought about it, the more Margesson fumed: it had been a truly scandalous act, an act in no way short of treachery, and the fullest report would go to Calcutta for onward transmission to Whitehall and St Petersburg. The Czar would be scarcely pleased. Margesson rumbled away inside: perhaps he should take over the full escort, relieving Tomislav of his command, even placing him in arrest until the fresh column took over at Dehra Dun, and recommend the relieving Brigade Commander to damn well keep him there...

Margesson rode slowly back towards the head of the column, watching the busy medical details and the preparations for the burial of the many dead. His face sombre, he stopped for a word of encouragement here and there. Lord Dornoch rode with him, sad-faced as he looked down at the Scots casualties, at his own dead now destined for the shallow graves beneath cairns of stones that were all they could be given in this hard and rocky land. All this, Dornoch detested: there would be letters to write as soon as the regiment reached mail facilities – letters, always hard to pen, to wives and mothers on Speyside and in the little town of Invermore, home depot of the 114th. So many who would not go back when the next trooping season came round and the *Malabar* sailed from Bombay for Portsmouth Hard... Dornoch, with an effort, switched his mind to present duty: there was much to do, much reorganisation of companies to be worked out with Black when he could be spared from his duties as Brigade Major to turn his mind to those of Adjutant of the Royal Strathspeys. More immediately, it was only too obvious that the Brigadier-General was in immense pain: Dornoch made it his business to urge him to have his wounds attended to. Though reluctant to take medical attention from those worse hurt, Margesson agreed at last; a pain-racked General might well be no use to his men at a time of difficulty. Dornoch sent word for Sergeant-Major Corton, who attended personally. The torn, blood-soaked khaki-drill tunic was removed with immense care while orderlies stood by with bandages and a sling.

It was close upon the hour accorded Colonel Gill by the time the graves were ready for the dead. Those to be buried would include the men of the advanced scouting party killed earlier. In the interval no gunfire had been heard; but Margesson indicated that he would delay the burial with its short committal service until contact with the Mounted Infantry companies had been made as promised. The allotted time having expired he was ready to lead out the column when the pickets to the west sent down word that Gill was coming in along the pass and appeared to be unaccompanied by the Cossacks guard or by the palanquin.

Margesson scowled and ordered the column to stand easy. Stony faced, he waited. Riding up, Gill made his report.

'No sign of anyone, sir. I went as far as I thought fit. Had they been there, I must have overtaken them.'

'Good God man, they can't have vanished into thin air!'

Gill shrugged, giving no answer to a self-evident truth. Margesson breathed hard down his nose, seemingly at a loss to know what he should do next. He did not doubt that Gill had extended his search far enough: the palanquin could proceed at no more than a slow walking pace. Looking around as if for some God-given inspiration, he saw Lord Dornoch in conversation with James Ogilvie, now remounted. Dornoch, catching Margesson's eye, rode his horse forward.

'Sir, Captain Ogilvie carried out a patrol in this part of the pass some while ago. He believes there is a track leading off, not far back to the west–'

'Why didn't he say so earlier?'

'I'm sorry, sir,' Ogilvie said. 'It was not a recent patrol, and I've only now picked up the landmarks–'

'Very well, Captain Ogilvie. Do you suggest Count Tomislav may have taken this track?'

'Yes, sir–'

'Then perhaps you can also explain *why*!'

'I can't do that, sir. I reported only because if the Cossacks are not in the pass, then they may–'

'Yes, yes. Where, precisely, is this track, Ogilvie?'

'As far as I remember, sir, no more than perhaps half a mile back beyond the bend. It's not immediately visible from the pass itself – there's an extended outcrop of rock acting as a cover, and from the pass it blends into the background.'

'Where does it lead to?'

'I've not been along it, sir, but it leads north, in the direction of Mardan.'

'And you suggest Tomislav's there, do you?'

'I suggest it's the only possibility, sir.'

Margesson said tartly, 'I still ask why.' He swung round on Black. 'Well, Brigade Major? Any ideas?'

'None, sir.'

'You're a lot of help!' Margesson said angrily. 'Let me see the maps – *is* this track mapped, Captain Ogilvie?'

'No, sir.'

'But it's penetrable?'

'For a little way at least, sir.'

Margesson blew out his breath and frowned. Then he said crisply, 'Very well, gentlemen, the track exists apparently, therefore it must be investigated, though I see no damn reason why Count Tomislav should hide himself in it, unless he means to give us the slip – which isn't likely! Lord Dornoch, if you please, detach Captain Ogilvie. He and his company will take over sufficient horses from Colonel Gill, and ride back. Captain Ogilvie?'

'Sir?'

'Your orders will be similar to Colonel Gill's – that is, you will bring back the palanquin if you should find it. If you do not, and I shall give you two hours, then you rejoin the column.'

'Yes, sir. And the guns?'

'You shall take the guns. The guns, of course, remain under the orders of Major Barrington in action, but I wish it to be clear that you command your company and are responsible to me alone.' In something approaching an echo of Bloody Francis Fettleworth, Margesson added, 'In my view, infantry is best handled by infantrymen even when mounted – and not by gunners.'

Ogilvie saluted and turned away. Riding back along the pass, he called for Colour-Sergeant MacTrease and passed the orders. As quickly as possible the exchange of horses was made; uncomfortably, incongruously in their kilts, B Company of the Royal Strathspeys moved to the rear past the Brigade Commander, in something approaching column of squadron though no self-respecting cavalryman would have recognised it as such. As the Brigadier-General returned his salute, Ogilvie saw that his face was grey and drawn with pain, though he appeared more comfortable with his arm in a sling.

Moving past the ready graves, the

mounted company, virtually holding on by their horses' ears in many cases, rode with all possible speed for the concealed entry off the pass.

The way ahead, hot and still under a burning sky, seemed totally empty. The only sounds were their own: the hoofbeats of the brigade horses, the rattle of rifles and bayonets, the voices of the mounted men, at ease now that Captain Black had been left behind. Ogilvie rode with Barrington, the gunner major, a monosyllabic man whose brief conversation had already indicated a clear but dangerous wish to engage the Russian artillery. Ogilvie's response to that had been that Count Tomislav was hardly likely to provoke action.

'Then why has he gone off on his own, Ogilvie?'

'That, we'll find out.'

'Yes, and perhaps with shot and shell!'

Ogilvie laughed. 'Oh, I think not, Major. He's very likely on his way to rejoin, after doing what he thought best to safeguard the Grand Duchess.'

Barrington had merely grunted, and thereafter had ridden in a morose silence, turning in the saddle now and again to look down upon his mule-borne artillery, and the native drivers urging the animals on with sticks and sharp cries, prodding from behind, keeping them in line when they appeared anxious to wander off the track. Ogilvie kept a close watch upon the time: he would turn back in two hours precisely, with or without the palanquin, though he knew its non-appearance would cause the greatest consternation to the whole column. Meanwhile Count Tomislav seemed to have gone to ground like a fox. It was a total mystery, inexplicable. Ogilvie glanced sideways at Major Barrington, riding stolidly along: rock-faced, with a heavy chin and hair growing low on his forehead, he was a man of little imagination beyond the carnage of an artillery barrage. He was obviously feeling none of the unease that was now beginning to visit James Ogilvie. It was almost a physical feeling, brought about partly by the stark fact of the mysterious disappearance of two squadrons of Cossacks with their entire supply train and partly by the geographical aspect of the terrain through which they were now riding. This was grimly awe-inspiring: the sides of the track rose sheer and high, much higher than the peaks of the main pass eastwards.

As the height increased to the right and left even the sun was cut off: the floor of the pass became a place of shadows, grey and eerie and, though claustrophobic and airless, a great deal cooler so that as they went on the day's sweat began to dry out from their clothing. Ogilvie, accustomed as he was to the ways of the Frontier provinces and their tribal inhabitants, and to the track-lore of the district, could find no sign of recent passage. This was not entirely surprising, for the ground was rock hard and the vegetation scant: but he would have expected some indication, even if only some spillage of animal feed from the supply train as the mules were urged along behind the palanquin and the riders.

Ogilvie was about to order the return to the column when Barrington gave an exclamation of surprise and jerked his revolver from its holster.

Ogilvie looked at him. 'What is it, Major?'

'I saw a movement, or I'm pretty sure I did. Ahead there – d'you see?'

'I don't see anything.'

'It's stopped. Over by that jag of rock just to the left of the track.'

'I still don't see it.'

'Lying low,' Barrington said. 'Inference –

decidedly not friendly! I'll jerk it into life.' Bringing up his revolver quickly, he fired. It was like a clap of thunder in the close confines of the pass: the high whine of the bullet ended in flying splinters of rock, but there was no other movement. Barrington rode his horse ahead, his revolver cocked and Ogilvie close behind him. Coming right up to the rock the gunner Major called sharply to the apparently empty air, bidding anyone taking cover to show themselves at once. There was no response, and Barrington rode his horse forward, heading it around the side of the rock. Ogilvie saw his sudden start of surprise and, following round, was confronted by a totally unexpected sight: a young white woman, little more than a girl, with long fair hair wound round her head and wearing the blood-stained jacket, cloak and riding boots of a Cossack.

'Well, I'll be damned!' Barrington! said, keeping the strange figure covered with his revolver. 'What d'you make of this, Ogilvie?'

'It seems we're on the track, doesn't it? I don't like it, though.' Ogilvie addressed the young woman, who was deathly pale and terrified. 'Who are you? What's happened – tell me, quickly!'

There was a swallowing movement in the long, delicate throat, a feverish look in the eyes. 'You are from the British force?' The English was good, though heavily accented, not in the same class as Count Tomislav's. 'I think I see you, yes?'

'Yes. Tell me what happened! Where's Count Tomislav, and the Grand Duchess?'

'They are gone. All gone.'

'Gone? What d'you mean, woman – gone?' This was Barrington, hard and heavy. The girl struggled to say more, but her eyes filled with tears, and she turned away weeping, her hands covering her face. Ogilvie, giving Barrington a warning look, slid off his horse and went towards her. He took her by the shoulders and made her face him, taking her hands gently from her face.

He said, 'We've come to help. What happened – and who are you? Why are you dressed like a man, a soldier? Come, you must tell me, and as quickly as you can.'

She gave her head a shake, biting her lower lip till the blood ran. Impatient, knowing that time could be running out too fast, Ogilvie tightened his grip on her shoulders till she gave a sudden cry. 'Tell me,' he said, his voice harsh now, 'or it will be my duty to make you!'

She seemed to stiffen, to come to terms with her own duty. She said, 'I shall try. Who are you?'

'Captain Ogilvie, of the Queen's Own Royal Strathspeys.'

She nodded, her face haunted by some fearful memory. She said, 'I am Countess Denarov, a lady in waiting to the Grand Duchess Sergius. Captain Ogilvie ... there was a terrible attack, an attack of dreadful ferocity.'

'The Pathans?'

'Yes.'

'How? Why did Count Tomislav leave the column? Quickly, now!'

The story came out piecemeal, accompanied by bitter crying. The girl – Ogilvie judged to be no more than nineteen or twenty – had seen much death in the last couple of hours and it was all much too recent. Count Tomislav, it appeared, had made an error of judgement – or had been swayed by an overdose of arrogant pride: he had pulled his Cossacks and the palanquin back to the rear of the brigade, fighting his way through the ranks of the Border Regiment, in what must have been an attempt to stand aloof, keeping his royal charge as far as possible from the attacking

Pathans, with the whole body of the British brigade between her and the enemy. As he listened, Ogilvie went cold with anger at the sheer stupidity: Tomislav, for all his fighting ardour, his tough Cossack training and his hauteur, knew nothing of the Frontier. The moment he had extricated himself from the British lines, the moment he had started for the rear and come around the bend in the track, out of sight of the heavily engaged British troops, the Pathan had struck. The natives had come swooping like a horde of vultures from out of the sky, dropping down from the peaks on to the very backs of the startled Cossacks, surrounding the palanquin and its close escort, rounding up the terrified attendants of the supply train. It had been, the girl said, an enormous force, outnumbering the Russians by more than ten to one, and they had had no chance. Ogilvie, in retrospect, understood why the Pathan resistance to the British charge had been somewhat less than normal, less than might have been expected: they had got what they wanted, using their hidden striking force held in reserve behind the peaks, and the British had not mattered very much.

This was going to be a bitter blow for

Brigadier-General Margesson.

'Go on,' he said.

'We were herded like goats, all of us, into the side pass, each one of us with many guns and bayonets behind us. We were brought to this place, moving very fast, too fast for many men and women, who fell.'

'And were made to get up?'

'Were picked up and carried in many cases. None were left, not even the dead.'

Ogilvie nodded, appreciating the need of the Pathans to leave no tell-tale traces: along the track he had not seen even any droppings from the horses and mules. Such, no doubt, would have been shovelled up. 'And then?' he asked.

Her hands covered her face once more, and her shoulders shook. Ogilvie watched the running tears in sympathy. Then she took her hands away and faced him. 'We were brought to Golgotha,' she said simply. 'Come and I shall show you, Captain Ogilvie.'

She turned away from the jag of rock and indicated the dark mouth of a cave concealed behind another rock shield, a cave-mouth lost in the gloom of the high-sided, sunless pass, a place that might never have been remarked by any passing body of soldiers. Ogilvie gave a shiver, and glanced at Barrington: the gunner's face was emotionless except for a small twitch at one corner of his mouth. They both knew they were about to find horror. Ogilvie looked around: MacTrease had halted B Company some twenty yards clear. Ogilvie called to him.

'Hold the men where they are, Colour-Sar'nt. Give us five minutes. If we're not back then, you'll advance.'

'Aye, sir.'

Ogilvie took the arm of the young Countess and, with Barrington close behind, went towards the cave-mouth, passing into deep darkness as soon as he was inside. The girl asked, 'You have matches?'

'Yes—'

'And I have a candle.' She brought it out from a pocket, and Ogilvie struck a match to light it. Cupping the flame with his hands he moved ahead slowly, feeling cautiously with his feet. The floor of the cave was smooth rock: the roof seemed high, the extent immense. The candle's flame showed no sides, no far end. Instead it showed death, death all around, and in total silence. Everywhere men, mules and horses lay – and women. Shot, bayoneted, knifed – all stone cold dead, proud Cossacks and lowly Russian peasants from the supply train, all motionless together in heaps, in spreading pools of blood. Ogilvie found himself shuddering uncontrollably: Golgotha, an apt description! *A place of Golgotha, and dead men's bones* ... He wanted nothing so much as to get out and away in good clean daylight, but humanity dictated the search for any living persons. He moved back to the mouth, and called to MacTrease. The Colour-Sergeant came in, caught his breath as he saw what the candle showed him. Together with Barrington and MacTrease, Ogilvie moved among the corpses, looking closely, feeling, where the wounds were not so obvious as to show death unmistakably, for heartbeats. He found not one person, not one animal alive. The killing of the Russians could no doubt be put down to military expediency: the slaughter of the horses and mules was killing for killing's sake, unnecessary and terrible. The commissariat carts were strewn everywhere, toppled and emptied of their stores. The Russian artillery had gone. The palanquin, its canopy stove in and the silken hangings bloodstained, was lying empty on its side. The place itself was death incarnate. There was no sign among the corpses of Count Tomislav: the girl explained that he had been taken away with the Grand Duchess. 'It was she they wanted, of course – those Pathan murderers. They took her away, tied to the back of a horse. I do not know where they went ... except that it was along the pass, in the direction opposite from where you came yourself, and they took the guns with them.' Her voice faltered: she was close to fainting, and no wonder. The search ended at last, they left the dead alone and emerged into the pass. Ogilvie looked with compassion at Countess Denarov.

'You?' he asked. 'How did you escape?'

'I pretended death. I crawled beneath a heap of Cossack dead ... it was horrible, so horrible!' Her eyes were staring, seeing yet a sight she would possibly never forget. 'In so doing, Captain Ogilvie, I ... escaped other things.'

'The other women – they were–'

'Yes, all of them, before they were slaughtered. Not the Grand Duchess, nor I. I had managed to hide myself, for long enough to take the uniform from a dead Cossack. Then, having escaped such a terrible thing, I crawled in amongst the dead as I told you,' She stared around the pass. 'What do you do now, Captain Ogilvie?'

Ogilvie shook his head, glancing at the Gunner Major. Barrington said, 'Well, we're a damn small force, Ogilvie, but clearly time's important now. If we don't pick up the trail quickly, they'll simply vanish.' He waved a hand around. 'It's a damn big area, I needn't tell you that!'

'You need not!' Ogilvie looked up towards the skyline of the peaks: he saw no-one, no rearguard left behind to harass a pursuit: that could show itself later, however. Making his decision he said, 'Right, we'll advance and try to pick them up, then hope to shadow them.'

'Until when?' Barrington asked sardonically.

'Until the column comes up behind, Major—'

'You can't make decision for the Brigadier-General, my dear fellow!'

'True, but I've no doubt he'll order the brigade in.' Ogilvie turned to MacTrease. 'Colour-Sar'nt, detail an escort of four and a lance-corporal. They're to ride back with the Countess, and report to Brigade.'

'Sir!'

'They're to tell the Brigadier-General, I'm advancing north along the pass in pursuit of the Grand Duchess Sergius and Count Tomislav. I'd appreciate reinforcements as soon as possible. That's all.'

MacTrease gave a swinging salute and, turning about smartly, shouted the orders for the detail. His voice was almost frightening as it broke the intense silence of the deep pass.

Chapter 8

'You're a brave young woman, Ma'am, with the stomach of a fighting soldier.' Brigadier-General Margesson looked with much approval at the Countess. 'More than I can say for ... no, no, I'll not go on. Forgive me. You've seen too much for any woman.' He gestured to Black. 'See she's given every comfort possible, Brigade Major, and fed as required.' Margesson, deciding to leave for the moment the questioning of the Countess in regard to the apparent mystery surrounding the Grand Duchess – this, though urgent enough, was not of first importance currently – conferred with his assembled colonels, one of them now being Major John Hay, second-in-command of the Royal Strathspeys, acting in the room of Lord Dornoch temporarily appointed Chief of Staff to Brigade. There had been consternation when the detail had ridden in, covered with dust that sweat had turned to a sticky yellow mud. The lance-corporal's report had made the anxiety a good deal worse.

'I'm not convinced,' Margesson said, 'that it would be desirable to send in the brigade at this point. You may well ask why: I say it could be a wild goose chase. The damned Pathans could be anywhere – right in the hills, and bugger the passes! As it is, we're free to move in any direction.'

'But which?' Dornoch asked impatiently. 'Isn't *any* direction only too likely to be another wild goose chase, sir?'

'Certainly. But I'm unwilling to commit the whole brigade in any one direction as things have turned out. We don't want all our eggs in one basket–'

'Sir, I have a company of mine advancing alone into what may well prove the greatest danger, great slaughter–'

'I know, Dornoch, I know. I sympathise. I detest risking men's lives as much as you do, and I detest even more sending inadequate forces into admitted danger. But Ogilvie has the guns with him, which we have not now – and frankly I must make the point that our first objective is to recover Her Imperial Highness. All my thoughts, all my decisions, must be directed towards that one end. I know you'll understand that. Now the maps again, if you please, Colonel.'

His face grim, Dornoch pulled the rolled-up maps from their metal canister. The Brigadier-General pored over them when Dornoch had spread them out on the trestle table, tracing lines with a forefinger, frowning in concentration. Dornoch knew what Margesson had in mind; routes that crossed, routes that merged ... an outflanking movement – always provided the guesswork was too brilliant to be true – could work. *Could!* But Dornoch had no liking for guesswork, for making deductions and assumptions without at least some basis to work upon. And if Ogilvie and a whole company of the regiment should perish as had those unfortunate Cossacks and their followers, then in Dornoch's view they would have been badly let down by the stupidities and misjudgements that fighting soldiers were always accustomed to associate rightly or wrongly with the Staff.

'Give them time, Major,' Ogilvie said.

Barrington's response was ominous: 'Time! Your detail will have reached Brigade four bloody hours ago – if they weren't gunned down on the way! Whatever the reason, Ogilvie, they're not coming in.'

'Then we continue on alone – that's all.'

'All right, all right! I'm not complaining, just explaining. Don't forget to bury me with my head to the east, I'm superstitious about that.'

Ogilvie smiled. 'I'm grateful for your support, Major. You realise, of course, that I'm in no position to give you or your battery orders?'

'You mean I can turn tail. Well, I'm not going to, you know that–'

'Yes.'

'I'm a bloody fool, but there it is,' Barrington said with a short laugh. 'I have a wife and child to support and no private means, or none to speak of, anyway. I have a need of the army. If it weren't for that...'

'You'd come anyway.'

Barrington replied with a vulgar noise. 'Granddaughters of the Queen-Empress ought to know a woman's place is in the home, not the hills. I can't see grandmother moving far from the palace without two battalions of servants plus carriage, bath and bed!'

'Which in point of fact the Grand Duchess more or less has – or had.' Ogilvie rode on, a prey to anxious thoughts. He pondered, not for the first time that day, on the

145

Countess Denarov, the Grand Duchess's lady-in-waiting: she at any rate had appeared to be in no doubt about the Grand Duchess's identity. That could be a pointer to quell the doubts that had plagued Margesson; on the other hand it might mean nothing at all. As Barrington had said when Ogilvie had raised the matter earlier, the Countess Denarov was presumably loyal to her country's aims and ambitions and resulting intrigues. It was, Barrington had said, all in the lap of the gods and their own lot was merely to plod on ... Ogilvie turned to look down the line of unaccustomed horsemen. Feed they now had in plenty, thanks to the Pathans having left behind much of the Russian commissariat; there was adequate food for the men also, but there was a sad lack of the kind of medical supplies saddle-sore, kilted Highlanders more at home on their own two feet were going to need by nightfall!

Dornoch's guess as to the Brigadier-General's intention had been a good one: Margesson was going to head east as far as the jointure with a track that according to the maps circled down from the north below Peshawar, a track that could quite possibly link with the unmapped one that Ogilvie had taken. Once there, he would make further appreciation. When the column moved out again, Margesson requested the presence of the Countess Denarov. Provided with a horse, the Russian girl rode with the Brigadier-General and Lord Dornoch, a striking and attractive and most unusual figure in her Cossack's uniform. Margesson, a hot-blooded man unaccustomed to seeing women riding astride, kept his eyes to the front in some embarrassment. Formally he asked the Countess if she was being well looked after.

'Very well looked after, General,' she answered.

'Good! Should you have any further requirements, or any complaints, please don't hesitate to tell my Chief of Staff, Lord Dornoch.'

'Thank you,' she said demurely. 'This I shall remember.'

'Good,' Margesson said once again. He cleared his throat noisily, pinched at his moustache. 'Countess, I have questions to ask, as my duty demands. You are not, of course, obliged to answer them, but I ask you to bear in mind that your country and mine are acting in concert upon this occasion. I, as well as Count Tomislav, have the responsibility for the Grand Duchess Sergius.'

'This I know, General.'

He nodded. 'Therefore any help you can give will be much appreciated, not least by Her Majesty Queen Victoria.'

'I understand. I shall help.'

Margesson looked relieved. 'I'm so glad, Countess. You have, I think, already told me all you know about the seizure by the Pathans.'

'Yes.'

'I'll not ask you to repeat that.' Margesson paused, cleared his throat again, wondering how best to phrase his pressing questions. He said, 'What I wish to ask you, Countess, will be in general terms rather than precise ones.'

'About Her Imperial Highness, the Grand Duchess?'

'Er – why, yes! May I ask what made you assume that, Countess?'

She said, 'Because I am not a soldier but a lady-in-waiting, and would therefore–'

'Quite, quite!' Margesson smiled, wiped sweat from his face as the hard metallic sun scorched down on the pass. Soon that sun would reach its zenith, climbing to a direct assault upon the helmeted heads. 'As a lady-in-waiting, you will naturally have a close acquaintance with Her Imperial Highness, and it is in her that I'm interested – naturally. I would have liked to have had the honour of being presented ... but Count Tomislav was opposed. D'you happen to know why that was, Countess?'

'I am sorry. I do not.'

Sharply, Margesson looked sideways. There was an uncompromising quality in the voice, such as he had not expected. He tried again, 'I commanded the Guards regiment in London. You will understand the inference.'

'Oh yes, I understand, General.'

'Then–?'

'I do not know why the Grand Duchess would not meet you. She did not say. I do not doubt that Count Tomislav told you what was true–'

'Do you know what he told me?' Margesson's voice was sharp now.

Countess Denarov smiled. 'I do not. But he will have told you something, and he is a man of truth and honour.'

'Really!' Margesson snapped. 'I'm delighted to hear it.' The Countess shrugged but made no answer. Dornoch, riding on her other side, was aware of a strong personality, one fitting the Cossack uniform she wore. Margesson was meeting his match: this young woman would be careful what she gave away. They rode on for a while in silence. The pipes and drums had started playing again and the column by Dornoch's order was marching at ease, though not unwatchfully, protected by the pickets on the flanks, high above the snail-like progress of the brigade. Dornoch watched one of the pickets ahead, coming down to the pass on relief: running, sliding, zig-zagging, descending at the rush in case of the sudden bullet in the back from a hidden Pathan rifle, his descent covered by the fresh picket on the heights. Dornoch looked across the Countess at Margesson: the Brigadier-General seemed to be struggling with himself, anxious, clearly, to come out with a great deal but doubtful of its wisdom. Then he tried again, cautiously.

'It's up to me to get the Grand Duchess away from the Pathans. Also Count Tomislav – he's officially in my charge too, whether he likes it or not. This is serious business, Countess, and not only on account of the Grand Duchess's physical safety as a human being. What I mean is,

half the civilised world is going to be concerned. I suppose you realise that?'

'Do you not over-dramatise, General?'

Margesson's face was a picture. 'No,' he
snapped, 'I do not! Surely you must realise
that importance attaches to the Grand
Duchess's mission to Katmandu? She's
scarcely going there to play skittles, Ma'am!'
He rode on angrily, then calmed himself. 'It
would be of some help if you were to tell me
exactly what her mission involves.'

'I do not know this. I am sorry.'

'You know nothing?'

'Nothing.'

'Very well, Ma'am, I have no more to ask
you. I suggest you continue resting, for the
march will be long.' Stiffly, Margesson
saluted. Dornoch rode away with the Countess, escorting her back to the commissariat
cart that had been cleared for her, and fitted
with a seat and a rough canvas canopy.
Handing the horse to an orderly and the
lady into the cart, Dornoch went back to the
Brigadier-General's side. Margesson returned his salute. He looked much put about.
'Confound the woman!' he said. 'I'm damn
sure she's not speaking the truth, Dornoch.
She's bound to know something, and if only
we knew what the mission was, we might be

able to make a fair guess at what the Pathans intended to do with the Grand Duchess – and even where they might have taken her, which is more to the point!'

'Time,' Dornoch suggested, 'may loosen her tongue.'

'Time! My dear fellow, that's just what we're likely to be short of, isn't it! I'll tell you one thing: I wish I had the advice of those political·wallahs! A mistake by Division – in retrospect – sending 'em with the column from Meerut...'

That night, when the brigade went into bivouacs, still enclosed by the surrounding hills and still some way short of the Jhelum River, special precautions were taken with the privacy of the Countess. A personal guard of sober-sided, married Scots privates was provided under a lance-corporal who would be directly responsible to the Brigadier-General for the lady's safety and seclusion. No chances were taken in regard to the column itself: the quarter-guard, the perimeter sentries, and the pickets in the hillside sangars were as fully alert as usual. Nevertheless, by some miracle the figure creeping down the sides of the pass, moving with extreme care from rock to rock, remained totally unseen: the first indication of any intruder's presence came when a woman's cry rang out in fear along the track, followed by the sound of rifle fire. On the instant the whole column, ever with half an eye on its arms and the likelihood of using them, came awake. Orders were called down the line of the 114th Highlanders and the Regimental Sergeant-Major himself went at the double towards the Countess's bivouac, a revolver in one hand and a claymore in the other. He found a man struggling ferociously outside the Countess's tent in the grip of the personal guard, a man whom, despite near nakedness, he recognised.

He stared in wonder. 'Count Tomislav!' he said. 'What is the meaning of this, sir?'

Tomislav, his face working, gathered saliva in his mouth, and spat. Cunningham moved aside just in time, with an exclamation of disgust. He said formally, 'I think sir, you had better come before the Brigadier-General.'

'Stupid peasant!' Tomislav sneered. 'That is what I wish.'

'It is, sir? I rather think, sir, you meant to attack the lady, and that's what I shall report. Now if you'll kindly come with me?'

Cunningham signed to the lance-corporal, who detached two of his men. Each man took an arm and the Russian was marched away in front of the Regimental Sergeant-Major's revolver, protesting loudly. In the moonlight Cunningham saw the unhealed knife wounds in the man's back and down one shoulder: Cunningham clicked his tongue. The Russky had suffered, right enough ... must have lost a lot of blood – but none of his arrogance by the sound of it! Marching smartly along the track towards Brigade, the Regimental Sergeant-Major gave the step with a certain amount of glee.

'Left ... left ... left, right, left! Smart now, pick up the step, Count Tomislav, sir, and don't *dawdle.*' So I'm a stupid peasant, am I, he thought to himself, we'll see about that! Coming up to where Margesson was standing with Lord Dornoch, looking down the line, Cunningham gave loud and per-emptory tongue: 'Prisoner and escort, *halt! Stand still!*' He approached the Brigadier-General and saluted. 'Sir! Count Tomislav, sir, apprehended whilst attempting to assault the Countess Denarov. Sir!'

'I made no attempt at assault–'

'Silence, Count Tomislav, sir!'

Margesson waved a hand. 'All right,

154

Sar'nt-Major. Explain what you found.'

'Sir!' Cunningham reported the facts as known. 'I witnessed no assault myself, sir, but the lady screamed.'

'Thank you, Sar'nt-Major. You may leave Count Tomislav in my charge now.' Margesson had his own revolver in his hand, pointed at the Russian. 'Dismiss the escort, if you please.'

'Sir!' Cunningham gave the orders and marched the escort away down the line of curious men. As his voice dwindled along the pass, Margesson curtly told Tomislav to sit down. Tomislav sat on a flat piece of rock, with Margesson looking down at him. Margesson said, 'Now your story, Count Tomislav.'

'I demand punishment for–'

'You will demand nothing. You have lost your charge, and you stand disgraced. Your men have killed my soldiers. I want a full explanation, and I want it now.'

'I shall explain nothing,' Tomislav said loudly, waving a hand in the air. 'I am a Colonel of Cossacks, answerable only to His Imperial Majesty the Czar, and–'

'I say you will explain, Count Tomislav. If you do not, I shall shoot you.'

Tomislav's mouth opened, then closed

again. He looked at Margesson, looked at Dornoch. He read a terrible determination. The revolver in the Brigadier-General's hand moved closer, pressure was coming on the trigger. Tomislav lifted a hand and dashed sweat from his forehead. 'You would shoot, you would kill me?'

'Like a dog.'

Count Tomislav shrugged, waved his hands in the air. 'Very well, I shall tell you what happened. My Cossacks were over-run–'

'That part, we know. Let us come to tonight. Why did you creep up on my column, like a thief, a thug?'

'I escaped. I escaped from the natives who had attacked–'

'Without the Grand Duchess, Count Tomislav?'

Tomislav scowled. 'Already she had been taken elsewhere – where, I do not know. I was powerless to help. I was going to be killed ... staked out in the sun beside the track, my uniform taken away, my body honey-smeared for the great ants to eat.' Tomislav was sweating again, his eyes staring as at some fearful mental image, a terrifying memory. 'So I escaped, as was my duty as a Russian soldier. Before they could stake me down I fought them with my bare hands – see, I have wounds to show.' He swung round displaying his knife-cut back and shoulder, then swung again to face Margesson. 'By that time, you see, the main body of natives had gone on with the Grand Duchess, only a small guard being left behind with me. I am strong, and I am Russian, and–'

'And fleet of foot!'

'That also, yes.' There was a hard anger in Tomislav's voice. 'Not only in retreat – my escape was no retreat, but an act of duty as I have said. When I had lost the pursuit in the hills, I made an assessment of where your soldiers might be, and my assessment was good. I come, as you can see.' He spread his hands. 'That is all, General. As to the Countess Denarov, this was coincidence. Earlier I had seen Cossack uniform, and assumed that one of my cavalrymen had also escaped. I made for the bivouac, to speak privately with him first–'

'Why, Count Tomislav? Why privately?' Margesson's voice was cold. 'Had you some arrangement, some accommodation with your attackers, that you–'

'I had not!' Tomislav's eyes shone bright in the moon's light, bright and hard and angry.

'I am a Russian officer and an aristocrat. I do not make accommodations with bandits. I wished to speak privately in order to ascertain the position before having words with you, General. I consider that a natural desire, if you do not!' He added, 'There was no assault, just fright to cause the screaming. Myself, I was as surprised as the Countess Denarov.'

Margesson nodded. 'I'll accept that, unless the Countess should give it the lie when I ask her–'

'Which she will not!'

'For your sake, let us hope not. You have explained, Count Tomislav, but you've not satisfied me yet. I wish to know more about the Grand Duchess, and I wish to know in precise terms what her mission is, and yours. What does the Czar intend in Katmandu, Count Tomislav?'

The Russian stared back at him, sneering now. 'My orders are secret,' he said. 'And you are a fool to think I would reveal them!'

'You refuse to tell me, then?'

'I refuse, yes. Shoot me if you wish. To do so would be catastrophic and would shake your Raj to its foundations when the world knows you killed a Russian officer who refused to act the traitor, General.' He laughed. 'You have gone too far. A little earlier, you could have shot me and explained it away as a mistake, a shot at a man who had – as you thought – invaded your camp. But not now.'

'If I were you, Count Tomislav–'

'If you were me, you would not talk about *your* orders. As it is, you are not me. You are here to obey your government, who has ordered you to act as my escort. I suggest you pay more attention to those orders, and not ask for mine.'

'I think you need a lesson in good manners,' Margesson said, fuming in frustration. 'Very well, then, for now you'll not talk. I think you will do shortly. At dawn the march will be resumed. You will march under escort, Count Tomislav, half naked as you are now, and with handcuffs. What's more you'll march smartly.' He turned to Lord Dornoch. 'Have him put in irons,' he ordered abruptly. 'Bread and water diet!' He felt a shade happier: today's breakfast would include no kedgeree for Count Tomislav.

Chapter 9

Count Tomislav was in the care of Colour-Sergeant Burnett and an escort of four: Burnett had been fully briefed by the Regimental Sergeant-Major, still smarting under the appellation of stupid peasant.

'You'll teach him we're not stupid peasants in the British Army, Colour Burnett.'

'Aye, I'll do that, sir.'

'No spite mind – just an insistence on smartness.'

'Just smartness, sir.'

'Carry on, Colour Burnett.'

Burnett was now enjoying himself. Count Tomislav, fallen in between the escorting privates, grinning men as pleased as their Colour-Sergeant, was made to march as smartly as the wearing of handcuffs would allow. This was not easy; to march without swinging the arms was always something of a strain. Count Tomislav's buttocks rode up and down, his feet kept the pace.

160

'Left ... left ... left, right, left! Head up, Count Tomislav – *sir* – shoulders back, if you please!' Burnett's voice carried clear down the column. 'Keep that paunch – beg pardon, stomach – keep it *in,* sir! You're not *pregnant* yet, sir!'

The heat was cruel: Tomislav longed for his horse, thirsted for water, hungered for the good breakfast he had not had. The British were pagans, Philistines, brutes and sadists: their laughter was too loud, would not in the Russian Army be permitted on the march. Tomislav scowled blackly. The British were degenerate, had no discipline, were over-friendly as between officers and N.C.O.s. He hated them with much intensity; but he kept the step, fearful not so much of Burnett's tongue *per se,* as of his own resulting fury. Running parallel with the pain of his indignity, and of his superficial knife-wounds now attended by the British doctor, were horrifying speculations on what his fate was to be when he returned to St Petersburg with his mission unaccomplished and the Grand Duchess lost. Czar Nicholas was not an easy man to placate.

As the sun rose to a cruel noon, the men were halted and fallen out to rest in the shade of the rocks and scrubby bushes, and to have their meal and an issue of water. The contents of the individual water-bottles had gone by this time, and the twice-daily ration was being issued from the tanks borne by the commissariat wagons. Margesson, at his luncheon table with Lord Dornoch, was uncommunicative: it was an unsociable meal and Dornoch was not sorry when it was broken into by a shout from one of the lofted pickets.

'Men in sight, approaching along the pass from the east!'

It was Cunningham who answered from the resting line. Dornoch heard his shout: 'Identify, Lance-Corporal Stock?'

'I believe they're ours, sir. A patrol maybe.'

Dornoch's heart leapt. Cunningham called out again. 'Captain Ogilvie, is it?'

'No, sir. An *English* patrol.'

Cunningham waved back, turned about and marched towards Black, who had been watching. Black nodded, returned the R.S.M.'s salute, and hastened to the Brigade Commander's side. Margesson said, 'Thank you, Brigade Major, we heard. Who the devil are they, I wonder?'

He got up from the table and stood with a napkin in his hand, staring eastward. After some delay, a mounted officer came into view, followed by what appeared to be a half-company of infantry of the line. The officer, a subaltern, rode in and approached the Brigadier-General, watched by hordes of speculative eyes. Dornoch, looking for the regimental insignia, saw the light infantry bugle on the subaltern's shoulder badges.

There was an exchange of salutes. Margesson asked, 'Who are you, and what are your orders?'

'Lieutenant Barnes-Wilson, 2nd Duke of Cornwall's, sir. My orders are to make contact with you—'

'Indeed! You're from Peshawar, I take it?'

'Yes, sir, from General Fettleworth—'

'And what the devil does *he* want – hey?'

'Sir, the brigade is to return to cantonments with the Grand Duchess Sergius.'

Margesson's face lost a good deal of its colour. 'Is it, by jove! Tell me, Mr Barnes-Wilson: is this General Fettleworth's unsupported notion, or does it come from higher up?'

'From higher up, sir. From Murree, and before that from the Viceroy.' The subaltern hesitated before dropping his final bombshell: the Brigadier-General's face was not a propitious omen. 'I understand there's been a meeting of the Cabinet of London, and that it is Her Majesty's wish that the Grand Duchess is brought back to a safer place.'

Margesson put his head in his hands and groaned. Dropping his hands again a moment later, he turned away and paced up and down, up and down beneath the high sun, before the silent group of officers. For a longish while he paced and thought, and when he turned back to Barnes-Wilson his expression was tight and grim. Making no bones about the situation, he said. 'Well, Mr Barnes-Wilson, the orders can't be obeyed. The Grand Duchess has gone, and God alone knows where she is now.' In a few words he explained, then went on, 'You'll not report that to Division. I intend to find the Grand Duchess myself and I don't want to start a full-scale Frontier war, which is what would result the moment General Fettleworth sent out the whole Division – and we still would not find the Grand Duchess any the quicker! What, precisely, were your orders, Mr Barnes-Wilson?'

'As I reported, sir. Then to ride back to cantonments with you.'

Margesson nodded, his eyes gleaming. 'Well, now you have fresh orders. You'll ride with me, but not back to cantonments. Small as they are, I can do with your reinforcements.'

Ogilvie reached out and laid a hand on the gunner Major's bridle. 'Easy!' he said, keeping his voice low. He raised his right hand in the air, turning to watch B Company and the mule-train with its guns come to the halt.

I thought I saw something ahead. A movement in that clump of bushes – d'you see?' He pointed: well to the north of Margesson's column now, he had turned eastwards some hours earlier after a probe along a junction of tracks had revealed a shoe cast from a horse. The shoe had not been of British pattern: possibly unjustifiably, Ogilvie and Barrington had decided to regard it as likely to be Russian if not Pathan. The new track had in due course led them clear of the high sides of the pass, out into a wide plateau set between distant hills that swept down from the Hindu Kush to the north. There was a sense of relief at being in open country, a lifting of the close oppression: here, for one thing, they could deploy to right and left, scatter, rather than present the compact target of a pass-bound force.

Barrington said. 'I don't see anything.'

'No, it's stopped now – or gone away.' Ogilvie looked around: it was not far off sundown, and he had to make the decision whether to bivouac or ride on through the night. Time, for the Grand Duchess, would be getting short. It was unlikely that she would be killed, certainly, but the longer the interval the less chance there was of catching up with her captor – if, indeed, they were on the right track in any case. Ogilvie had reached a decision to continue riding to the limit of the horses' endurance when he saw the slight movement again, and again drew Barrington's attention to it.

'Someone there, I'd swear to it, Major.' As if by mutual consent, neither had used field glasses: there could be value in not letting the enemy know he had been spotted. The halt could be for any number of reasons. Still Barrington failed to spot anything, and Ogilvie gave the order to ride on. Coming nearer the clump of scrubby growth, he looked again: this time both he and Barrington saw the vague outline of a brown body, naked but for a loin cloth, and with a curious gleam that indicated an oiled skin. At the same moment Colour-Sergeant Mac-Trease rode up the flank of the company and reported his own sighting.

'All right, Colour Major, we've seen it.'

'Orders, sir?'

'I don't know yet. He could be better left.'

Barrington shifted restlessly in his saddle; he was about to say something when there was sudden movement from the bushes, and the shining body was seen briefly, beating it fast to the rear. Ogilvie turned. 'All right, men,' he called. 'Bring him down smartly!'

The rifles crashed out, a single volley, somewhat ragged. Smoke drifted on a light breeze, sharp, acrid. The sound died away: the native was seen lying on the ground, still as death. MacTrease called an order and two men dismounted and ran across, followed by Ogilvie and Barrington on horseback. Sliding off their horses, they knelt by the man, whose eyes were rolling hideously. Blood was welling from the back and chest: he was not going to last more than minutes. Ogilvie wiped sweat from the face with his handkerchief, moved the long straggling hair away from the eyes. He spoke in Pushtu, urgently.

'Why were you watching?'

There was no answer.

'Who gave you orders?'

It was hopeless: the Pathan knew he was

about to die. Why should he speak? There was hatred in the face. Ogilvie stood up and stepped away from the body. A moment later the face contorted and there was a gush of blood from the lips, then the head lolled sideways. Ogilvie met Barrington's eye. 'Poor bugger,' he said.

Barrington shrugged. 'Siva, the Mahadeva outdid Vishnu. That's all!'

'Wrong religion, Major. He was a Mohammedan.'

'All the same thing in the end, isn't it?'

Ogilvie didn't answer. With the gunner he rode back to his company. 'We go on,' he told them. 'No bivouacs tonight.' He lifted a hand, waved towards the dead Pathan. 'My guess is, he was one of perhaps many scouts watching for a rescue party. If I'm right, we're getting warmer. Keep your eyes skinned for any more – they'll get harder to see as the sun goes down, of course, but keep on the alert. And next time, I'll do the shooting. We need the next one alive.' He turned to MacTrease. 'Carry on, Colour MacTrease.'

'Sir!' MacTrease's hand swung to the salute, and he rode down on the rear of the mounted company while Ogilvie and Barrington resumed the lead. They went on through the wide open landscape, finding their way by compass, heading always east towards distant Nepal along a little used track that now and again vanished completely on hard, rocky ground. Soon the sun went down in the western sky behind them, throwing back long shadows from the mountains through which they had come. It was a splendid sunset but one that Indian service had well accustomed them to: magnificent colours shot the darkening sky with green and purple, red and orange, giving the heavens a landscape-contour all their own. Alert as he was keeping, James Ogilvie found his thoughts moving across the seas to Scotland, to other glorious sunsets over the Western Isles when the sun sank below Tobermory to drench the Sound of Mull with fairy light or, farther to the eastward, to bring up the Duke of Argyll's great castle of Inveraray in granite grandeur beside the darkening waters of Loch Fyne. Riding on through the encroaching dark, he worried about the brigade, hoping that the escort had got through with the Countess Denarov. Anything might have happened, and only one thing was certain: no support was coming through from Margesson. Had men been sent, they would surely have overtaken them before they turned of along this east-ward-leading track. An assessment of future prospects seemed bleak enough: however great the difficulties, however dangerous, the retrieval of the Grand Duchess was vital. Obsessed with the need to keep going, Ogilvie was short with MacTrease when on reaching a stream he rode up to report the horses in need of rest.

'What about the men?'

'They're all right, sir, they'll manage. It's the horses, sir.'

'I'll halt to feed and water them. Then we move on.'

'They're dead weary, sir–'

'You heard the order, Colour-Sar'nt.'

'Sir!' Disapproval in his monosyllable, MacTrease saluted and turned away. The company halted, and feed and water was provided for the horses. Barrington was as unhappy as MacTrease, and said so plainly.

'We'll not move far without them, Ogilvie. They have to be respected, they're not machines.'

'They'll have to keep going, Major.'

'Flesh and blood – even animal – has its limits. You don't seem to know horseflesh.'

'I'm an infantryman.'

'Also a gentleman, Ogilvie. Gentlemen

know horses – or should!'

'Well, I'm sorry.'

Barrington gave a quiet laugh. 'You may be sorrier than you think, my dear fellow! I *do* know horses. I've served with the horse gunners – the field batteries, I mean, the heavy stuff. Our horses were splendid, pulling the guns and limbers as though they were no more than governess carts ... but they, too, had their limits. I never went beyond them, never. If I'd done so, I'd have had mutiny on my hands – led, what's more, by my Battery Sar'nt-Major!'

Ogilvie shrugged but paid no heed. The horses replenished, he gave the order to move out. Soon the moon was up, shining brightly on a deserted plateau, outlining trees and bushes and rocks in silver. The place seemed utterly deserted but for the British troops and their mounts: nothing moved anywhere apart from the occasional scurry of some small animal out of line of advance. The only sounds, too, were those peculiar to the mounted force, the creak of harness leather, the ring of shod hooves on rock, the rattle of rifles and bayonets laid across the saddles, plus from time to time the cry of a night bird, or the flap of great wings as vultures passed overhead searching for supper. It began to seem a hopeless quest, more useless by far than the needle in the haystack. Like that needle in its haystack, a Grand Duchess in tribal territory was a contradiction: Grand Duchesses were customarily in the midst of courts, servants, hangers-on, retainers, lovers. They were not alone, in terror of their lives!

The ride continued, men and horses growing wearier. Skin chaffed against leather, and bottoms bled, causing the Royal Strathspeys to curse their kilts, to curse the immediacy of the order that had sent them out un-trewed, not that in any event there would have been the trews to go round a whole company, since Mounted Infantry was normally formed in cantonments rather than on the march. Now, as Ogilvie had prophesied, it was becoming much harder, almost impossible, to pick out any lurking scout who would report their movement. The bright moon, however, helped; if it struck its light from a rifle or bayonet or long knife, the alarm might be given. But the moon failed to oblige, shedding its light on blankness and silence. Still Ogilvie rode the horses on, dead tired himself, and stiff from the unaccustomed saddle and the plodding, swaying motion. When dawn came up it found the men red-eyed and lolling upon their weary animals. Barrington was about to force Ogilvie's hand by halting his own gun-mules when he became aware of a sound, familiar to him but alien to the long-lasting silence, and sinister, coming from the right of the line of advance and some way ahead. No-one else seemed to have strength enough left to hear it, and for the moment nothing could be seen. But the sound was enough for Barrington.

'There's horsemen ahead!' he snapped, pulling his revolver from its holster. He thumbed the hammer back. 'Damn it, Ogilvie, wake up – you're tired out by your own damn obstinacy–'

'I'm not asleep, Major.' Ogilvie stared ahead: the sounds came closer, and soon figures were seen against the dark background of the foothills, horsemen riding down on the small column hell-for-leather, savage, turbaned men waving the long-barrelled jezails of the Pathans. Ogilvie stood in the stirrups. 'Colour MacTrease, scatter the men, get them into cover! Dismount! Major, I'd suggest you assemble your guns!'

Barrington nodded, pulled his horse round, and rode to the rear at the gallop, shouting for the guns. Ogilvie flung himself off his horse and ran with it on the bridle towards a rocky outcrop to his right. Mac-Trease, running like a demon and bellowing orders, had the men dismounted and making for what cover they could find when Ogilvie gave the word to open fire: there was a ripple of flame from the Scots and then the horsemen in the lead of the oncoming horde opened with the jezails. Bullets zipped across the track, whining past those of the Scots who were still seeking cover. By the guns Barrington, still mounted, went down from his horse as it dropped suddenly to its knees. He flew over its head to land heavily against a rock. A moment later Ogilvie saw the Major's body jerk into the air, and contort, and fall back limp. Then the real exchange of fire settled in, with the Scots keeping up a sustained barrage from their various points of cover as the Pathans swept down, some two hundred of them, to form a circular ride around the British soldiers, a ring of pounding hooves and dust interspersed with white puffs of gunsmoke.

Chapter 10

Crouched behind his rock, Ogilvie held his own fire, conserving his revolver cartridges until the Pathans closed the range; but the rifles were nicely in action, covering the assembly of the mountain guns under the orders of the dead officer's Battery Sergeant-Major. Within minutes Ogilvie heard the scuffle of loose stones and rocks as the N.C.O. crawled up on his stomach.

'Guns read, sir.'

'Right, Sar'nt-Major. No target for the moment – we'll wait till they bunch a little more.'

'If they do, sir. They're wily bastards.'

'I know that, but we've no rounds to waste.' Feeling helpless, Ogilvie watched as his Scots returned the Pathan fire. Their aim was sure: the Pathans appeared to be getting the worst of it, but the circle of pounding hooves was kept in being, gradually closing and keeping up the firing. Then, for no

175

immediately apparent reason, the circle broke, and the natives streamed away to form up in a ragged line on some rising ground to the Scots' left.'

'Now, sir, the guns?'

'They've got something up their sleeve,' Ogilvie said. 'They've seen the guns. They may be trying to draw our fire. We'll wait, Sar'nt-Major.'

'I could blast the buggers to Kingdom Come, sir, from here.'

Ogilvie nodded, felt his mouth caked dry with dust from the flying hooves. 'They're keeping us guessing. We're going to keep *them* guessing.' He rose from behind his rock, called out to MacTrease: 'Hold your fire, Colour MacTrease!'

A khaki-clad arm waved back. 'Aye, sir. What d'ye think they're after now, sir?'

'We'll wait and see,' Ogilvie called back. MacTrease went down into cover again, his rifle ready for the next attack. Ogilvie looked around in what had become a brooding silence, saw here and there between the rocks and bushes the splash of colour of the Royal Strathspeys' tartan. Some of the men lay in rigid, unnatural positions. It was the fortune of war, and before they had died, they had held the line: but Ogilvie's thoughts were bitter ones, an inner fury against the Russians for sending them into an unnecessary action. God alone knew what might have motivated Count Tomislav's arrogantly stupid action in breaking to the rear the day before. Whatever those motives were, they had been wholly responsible for many Scots' deaths.

Watching the Pathan line, Ogilvie saw some movement: the natives had drawn closer together and seemed to be conferring. Then a lance was raised: fluttering from it like a cavalry guidon was a white square of cloth.

'A flag of truce!' Ogilvie said wonderingly. 'Now what's the idea?' With the Battery Sergeant-Major, he waited, keeping in cover still. Four riders moved forward, coming down on the Scots' positions, walking their horses. They halted some three hundred yards off, and a shout came from one of them, a shout in Pushtu which Ogilvie was unable to catch. He was about to get to his feet and try to bring some sense and understanding into the situation when he felt the sudden hard pressure of the gunner N.C.O.'s hand on his arm. 'Look to your right, Captain Ogilvie, sir!'

Quickly, Ogilvie looked right. In that first

moment he saw nothing: then became aware that the very ground appeared to be on the move, undulating, creeping closer. A strong force of natives, rifles and bayonets glinting in the sun, was coming up, stealthy and silent, approaching bent double or on their stomach.

'Creeping bastards,' Ogilvie said harshly. 'All right, Sar'nt-Major, open with your guns, quick as you like now!'

'Sir!' The N.C.O. got to his feet and ran full pelt for his battery, shouting as he went, risking bullets. The apparent truce party galloped back to their own line, while the advancing native infantry rose and came on at the charge. To Ogilvie, they had the look of Pathans. A moment later, with a sharp series of cracks and puffs of smoke, the mountain guns opened, sending their bursts down on the advancing horde. Ogilvie, running for the battery, yelled at the Sergeant-Major to swing two guns to bear on the horsemen, who were now belting down from the left. Quickly the guns were swung: the aim of one of them was true and effective. There was an eruption of flame and chunks of rock plumb on the cavalry line, and when the air had cleared it was as though a giant's bite had cloven into them.

With the battery firing on both fronts at an impressive rate, Ogilvie joined his Scots on the ground, and with MacTrease formed them into two recumbent ranks, feet to feet and facing outwards. The rifles went into action, meeting both charges simultaneously, bringing the Pathans down in twos and threes but failing to halt the onrush of men and horses. A handful of riders jumped the line, hooves flying over the heads of the men: one took a bullet in the belly as a soldier quickly lifted his rifle, and went headlong, breaking its rider's neck. Two of the Scots moved into the lee of the dead animal, using it as cover against the advancing infantry, now so close that the guns were firing point-blank and causing terrible casualties. But heavily out-numbered as they were, the Scots could have little hope of winning through. Ogilvie getting to his feet to yell his company on and lead a counter-charge, was at once attacked by a tall, heavily-built native who seemed to rise up from the very ground to throw himself at the British officer's throat: hands like steel went around Ogilvie, throttling, squeezing the life from his body, but bringing his revolver up and into the man's thick chest, he used his last bullet. The man fell to the ground and Ogilvie, turning as he sensed another man behind him, caught a brief glimpse of the reversed rifle, its butt swinging like a club, just before it took him hard on the side of the head.

Ogilvie came round to intense pain and sickness, heard his own retching, felt a terrible giddiness as his body swayed and lurched as though aboard a small boat in a rough sea. More nausea came in waves as he opened his eyes: he saw dust and scrub, and rock, and a blinding light of many colours. He closed his eyes, felt the bile stir in his stomach. There was an animal smell in his nostrils, and he heard native voices chattering. His body, was constricted, there were ropes around him. Dizziness overcame him and he passed once again into unconsciousness. When he came to again, things were a little clearer, and recent events returned. There had been a débâcle, he had lost a lot of men, and currently, as he now realised, he was tied like a sack of flour to the back of a horse, going he knew not where. Into his restricted vision came a line of men in the kilts of the Royal Strathspeys, a line of captive Scots shambling along under the Pathan guns, some of them with bound hands being led along behind the victorious native cavalry. He saw Colour-Sergeant MacTrease, marching like a soldier yet, but with blood staining his khaki-drill tunic and his crimson sash, and a hopeless, outraged look in his eyes, seeing nothing but humiliation. The caravan of men and horses moved on: now and again there came a burst of native song, a sound of victory and high spirits, exultant and foreboding. The sun was past its zenith now and they moved through the heat of the afternoon, scorched and thirsty. After what seemed hours of pain and never-ending motion on the back of the horse, head to tail, the nature of the ground changed and they came thankfully into shadow, losing the terrible shafts of the sun. They were moving now between high sides, once again along a pass in the hills. For some time yet they plodded on, a silence falling over the Pathan escort, then at last there was a slowing of the movement and they stopped.

Rough hands pulled at the ropes binding Ogilvie. He slid to the ground in a heap, unable for a while to help himself. He heard MacTrease's voice: 'I'll see to the officer—' The voice broke off suddenly, and there was a gasp of pain and anger. Looking up,

Ogilvie saw the long, rusty bayonet held at the Colour-Sergeant's throat.

'It's all right, Colour MacTrease,' he called. 'I'll loosen up presently.'

The only response was in MacTrease's eyes: there was blood running down his throat, a trickle only, but a promise of what might come. Massaging life back into his limbs, Ogilvie got up from the ground. He reached out towards the horse for some support, and looked around, his head throbbing like a drum and caked with dried blood. A rough count of heads showed some sixty Scots on their feet, another ten still tied to the mules and horses, some badly wounded among them. A loss of around thirty men, a bitter pill. And though the guns were present, there was no sign of their crews...

Ogilvie felt a hand on his shoulder, and he was swung round roughly. A squat man confronted him, a man with immense shoulders and a deep, powerful chest, a man naked but for his loin-cloth, and rippling with muscle beneath a smooth oiled skin. There was a dun-coloured turban on his head, which came no further than Ogilvie's chest.

'You are the officer,' this man said, using Pushtu.

'Correct. What do you want?'

'I want information.'

'About what?'

'The British intentions in regard to the escort of the woman from Russia.'

Ogilvie stared back at the native. It seemed he had fallen into somewhat relevant hands, that the sudden attack from out of the blue had been no chance foray by a band of ordinary brigands. He gave his answer flatly: 'I shall tell you nothing. Who are you?'

The native shrugged. 'I? I am but the representative of my master.'

'And he?'

'The Nawab of Bandalpur.'

'Bandalpur!' Ogilvie was shaken. 'The Nawab is a good friend of the Raj—'

'Yes. Just so, Captain Sahib. That is why he has acted. The coming of the Russian woman is not in the interest of the Raj, and this the Nawab knows.'

'Has the Nawab's act been in our interest, then? Is the killing of soldiers of the Raj to be considered in the interest of the Raj? I do not understand you.'

The native said indifferently, 'Lives are cheap, of small account when weighed in the balance, Captain Sahib. As it was, it was you who fired first upon us, not us upon you. And when a flag of truce was raised, you fired upon that also.'

Ogilvie caught his breath: this was true! The ways of the Frontier were such that it was always advisable to get the first shot in – especially when the opposing side crept upon its stomach. His head throbbing with pain that clouded his thoughts, he said, 'I find Pathans strange bedfellows for His Highness the Nawab of Bandalpur. He may well consider the interest of the Raj to be his own. You and your fellows, on the other hand, are unlikely to do so! Can you explain this?'

The man smiled, watching Ogilvie like a hawk. 'I can explain. The Nawab has made promises to us which he will keep.'

'Money?'

'Money and lands, and a measure of his protection.'

'Which, in the balance of which you spoke, outweighs any consideration of the Pathans' customary enmity against the Raj?'

There was a mocking smile again. 'So. Just so!'

Ogilvie was silent, though scarcely from surprise: his years on the North-West Frontier of India had dulled his capacity to feel surprise for long. Expediency was the watchword of the native, be he high or be he low, be he Prince of British India or warring tribal leader. Ever the handsome bribe and, hand-in-hand with it, the knife in the back, with final victory to him who was mightier or faster to react in his own defence. All this would never change: in the meantime, it began to appear likely that he, James Ogilvie, mere Captain of Infantry, would shortly move close to the heart of what was indeed the most pressing problem, currently, of the Raj; and one that would entail more diplomacy than fighting skill.

He asked, 'Do I take it you are ordered to lead me to the Nawab himself?'

'No. This is not desired. The Nawab does not wish to be seen to be involved, or to be found with soldiers of the Raj under duress. You will give me the information that is sought, and I will take it personally to His Highness in Bandalpur.'

'And to the Grand Duchess Sergius?' Ogilvie asked slyly.

The native's eyes narrowed. 'Why do you ask this, Captain Sahib?'

'I think you know why – but no matter! You'll not tell me, any more than I shall tell you anything about the British intentions.'

185

He added with a show of indifference, 'If any information is to be given, it will not be to a Pathan, you may be sure of that, my friend!'

'There is time,' the native said, 'but not much time, for you to change your mind. I advise quick thought, less I grow impatient. Meanwhile you will join your men, and be very careful not to give me cause to shoot them.' He turned away and gestured to his tribesmen. These men moved forward and at bayonet-point the Scots were herded back against a sheer rock side, and made to sit cross-legged at its foot with the Pathan rifles covering them. All the tribesmen looked trigger-happy, only too anxious for an excuse to kill. Ogilvie knew that he himself would be safe for so long as the Pathans believed he might be made to talk: but any incautious move on his part would kill a Scot as surely as if he himself had squeezed the trigger. He found himself covered in sweat as he sank down beside MacTrease who, his expression dour and grim, told him briefly that he had had enough Pushtu to take in the drift of what the native spokesman had been saying.

'What do you make of it?' Ogilvie asked.

'One thing I know, sir, is this: if the bloody

Nawab wishes to remain on good terms with the Raj, he'll not want it known that his hired assassins gunned down our men!'

'You mean–'

'I mean, sir, that none of us are going to come out of this alive, to tell the tale after. That's what I mean.'

Ogilvie said, 'Yes, I'd got there too, Colour-Sar'nt.' His nails dug hard into his palms. 'God damn these power-mad native rulers and their bloody machinations! We should never have let them keep such power ... it's no wonder the Nawab so fervently supports the Raj!'

'A treasonable utterance, sir, if I may be so bold!' MacTrease chuckled. 'He's our gallant ally, Captain Ogilvie, sir!'

'One we can currently do without. A pound to a penny he's got the Grand Duchess tucked away in his blasted palace.'

'My own thought exactly, sir.' MacTrease frowned. 'What do we do now?'

'A display, I rather think of masterly inactivity, Colour-Sar'nt!'

'Well, now, I'd not be too sure. Yon brown bastard has an impatient look, Captain Ogilvie. He's not going to hesitate to kill some more men as soon as he sees the need for a hastener.'

'What do you suggest, then?'

MacTrease said, 'A wee yarn wouldn't hurt, sir.'

'Anything to keep him happy?'

'Aye...'

Ogilvie shook his head. 'I think not. It'd rebound too smartly. I'm going to play a waiting game. I've already dropped the hint – if you picked that up?'

'You'll talk to the Nawab? Is that it, sir?'

'That's it.'

'And you'll *really* talk to the Nawab, sir?'

Ogilvie said, 'We'll cross that bridge if and when we come to it, Colour-Sar'nt.'

MacTrease sat in silence, looking dubious. He said warningly, 'It'll be touch and go. You'll need to assess the moment when yon bastard's losing his patience.'

'I'll be careful,' Ogilvie said quietly. 'I don't want to lose any more men. I've lost enough already...'

MacTrease turned and looked him squarely in the eye. 'You're never blaming yourself for that, sir! Och, I'll no' have that, Captain Ogilvie, nor will the men! You did what was right in the circumstances and no-one can blame you for making a fight of it. It's well understood, sir.'

'Thanks for that, Colour MacTrease. I'm

grateful.' Ogilvie paused. 'What happened –
to the gun's crews?'

'Slaughtered,' MacTrease said briefly.
'Every man...'

'And not buried.'

'Buried!' MacTrease gave a hard, bitter
laugh. 'Come now, Captain Ogilvie, sir, did
ye ever know the bloody Pathan to treat
British dead decently?'

The wait was a long one: the evening
shadows came down, and with them the
cold of the high hills, and the start of a wind
to whistle and probe along the pass. Still the
relentless rifles held steady behind the long
snaky bayonets, still the Pathan leader had
held onto his patience, waiting for the
insidious worm of uncertainty and anxiety
to loosen the British captain's resolve. That
didn't loosen; but it grew harder and harder
to maintain as the moans of the wounded
men came to Ogilvie along the pass, the
sounds from men who desperately needed
the care of a doctor. MacTrease was more
and more restive by his side, clearly more
and more apprehensive that at any moment
the bullets were going to fly. Steel nerves
were needed now: Ogilvie's held. Determined not to make the first move, he waited for

the Pathan leader's patience to give way: that would be his moment, the moment of most likely success, and at last it came.

It came very suddenly: a quiet command, and the crack and flash of a rifle close by. A bullet snicked the ear of the man, a private, on Ogilvie's left; for a moment the air was blue with Highland blasphemies. Mac-Trease whispered, 'Captain Ogilvie, for God's sake!'

All right, Colour-Sar'nt.' Ogilvie addressed the watchful Pathan, just visible in the last of the light. 'I shall talk, but only to His Highness in person.'

'You will talk to me, Captain Sahib.'

'Not so. Officers of the Raj speak to their equals, not to mercenary bandits. You know this, His Highness knows it and may well be expecting it. If I were you, I'd be very careful. You have said yourself, the Nawab is a good friend and ally of the Raj, and he is powerful. This too you know.'

'You will talk now, or my men will shoot. Already they are impatient–'

'That's obvious.' Ogilvie spoke with contempt, staring into the Pathan's eyes. 'You have my answer. I would advise that you don't take your revenge on my soldiers. His Highness will not be pleased. You Pathans, my friend, are not the only people to believe in *melmastia*. The Raj is equally fond of revenge, and has a long arm. It can and will reach out to Bandalpur, and His Highness will know that he will be held answerable for your actions by the powerful armies of the Raj, who will march from Nowshera, and Peshawar, from Mardan and Murree, to burn Bandalpur about His Highness' ears. You know that I speak with a strong tongue. Heed it!'

The Pathan scowled, but now had a look of uncertainty. Muttering to himself like some grotesque and animated caricature, he moved away, beckoning to some of his followers MacTrease whispered, 'Do you think he'll agree, sir?'

'I do. He'll be wallowing in sundry unpleasant thoughts. His Highness won't approve of being denied audience with someone who's agreed to talk – and never mind what the middleman says! Just wait and see.'

They went on waiting, shivering in the contrasting chill of night. Soon the Pathan leader came back, scowling still. Abruptly he said, 'So be it. I agree. We shall ride, Captain Sahib – you, your soldiers, my soldiers. Whether your soldiers live or die will depend only on your own actions, Captain Sahib.'

They rode through the night, with Ogilvie in the centre of a special escort of four and the squat leader behind, watchful with his jezail, and the rest of the Pathans closely guarding MacTrease and the men. They rode in silence, silence broken only by the horses' hoof-falls and by the whine of the wind out of Himalaya. As the dawn came up they breasted a rise in the pass, then rode out of its confining hills to be confronted with the broad aspect of the Indian plain, with the shining towers and minarets of the old city of Bandalpur sleeping beneath the climbing sun behind the thick defensive walls. Still in silence they rode down towards the gates, hearing from the far distance, clearly in the thin mountain air, the keening call of the muezzin.

As they approached more closely, armed men were seen behind the embrasures along the high walls; a tinny bugle sang out, and a few minutes later the great gates were opened, creaking on ancient hinges, to reveal a stately elephant bearing a curtained howdah on its back, and a mounted guard of the Nawab's private army. Moving with his escort into the smells and narrow alleys of the native city, Ogilvie heard with foreboding the reverberating thud as the gates were shut behind him.

Chapter 11

'The Grand Duchess is in good health, Captain Ogilvie.'

'Then Your Highness will permit me to see her?'

The native ruler shook his head, smiling. 'Not so. In time perhaps, but not now.' He sat on a thick cushion, his legs crossed at the ankles, staring at Ogilvie. The smile faded, leaving the fat, dark face enigmatic and threatening. Like his opulent but dirty palace, the Nawab smelled, a mixture of sweat, an over-indulgence in strongly-spiced foods, and bad teeth: the Nawab of Bandalpur was no British-educated Highness, no product of Eton or Sandhurst; he was a stranger to the colleges of Oxford of Cambridge. His ties with the Raj were not those of sentiment or association: they were those of expediency and a greedy ambition. He looked what he was: a hard bargainer, a man avid in self-interest, a man currently with a rich prize within his grasp.

Some of this Ogilvie knew, some of it he was well able to guess. It added up to a difficult task for a plain soldier; however well he might have come to know the more lowly native mind, the ruler of a princely state the size of Wales presented problems very different from those of daily regimental dealings with the natives in the Peshawar cantonment. Ogilvie needed time to make an assessment: immediately upon arrival inside the gates of the city he had been taken to the palace and brought before the Nawab, to be told firstly, with an oily smile, that his wounded soldiers would be treated and cared for against a day when their lives might become important, and secondly, with bald complacency, that the Grand Duchess Sergius was also in the palace and within the power of the Nawab. So far, nothing else had emerged.

Suddenly the Nawab asked, 'Where is the Russian, Captain Ogilvie?'

'The Russian? Which Russian, Your Highness?'

'Count Tomislav.'

Ogilvie stared. 'I understood you took him with the Grand Duchess?'

'He has escaped. It was intended he

should die. Before he could be killed, he got away from my soldiers.'

'I know nothing of that.'

'No matter.' The fat potentate waved his hand airily. 'He will be found again, and put to death.'

'Why put to death?'

The ruler chuckled. 'Why not? He is a marauder, a barbarian who intends no good to the great British Raj. Why should he not die? He is not important, Captain Ogilvie. The Grand Duchess is very important, is this not so?'

'Very important, Your Highness.' There was no point in denying the obvious; a heavy ransom demand was coming in any case. 'You know who she is, no doubt?'

'This I know. She is the granddaughter of Her Imperial Majesty, the great and good Queen Victoria, Empress of India.' Almost as a reflex action, the hairy face dipped in an obsequious motion: Ogilvie found it repellent; this man's loyalty was as deep as his treasure-chest and no more. Nevertheless he had to be pandered to, his blatant kidnapping of the Grand Duchess blandly regarded, at least for the present, as a kindly act for the good of the Raj.

Ogilvie said, 'This is correct, Your Highness. If you will hand the Grand Duchess over to me, I will see to it that she is taken in safety to Peshawar. I can also, I believe, promise Her Majesty's gratitude.'

The eyes glittered, a look of amusement. 'This gratitude will lead to a Companionship of the Most Exalted Order of the Star of India? Even, I might become a Knight Grand Commander of this noble Order, Captain Ogilvie?'

'It is possible, Your Highness,' Ogilvie agreed solemnly.

'Pish to the noble Order!' the Nawab said, giving a loud shout of laughter. 'I perform a great service for the Raj, and you suggest I am offered pieces of ribbon? Come–'

'What service do you perform, Your Highness?'

The Nawab's heavy eyebrows went up. 'You ask what service? Do I not restore the Grand Duchess to her grandmother the Empress of India, after extracting her from exploiters?'

'You intend, then, to restore her? May I ask, Your Highness, what are the wishes of the Grand Duchess herself?'

'She has not made them known,' the Nawab said.

'Then perhaps she doesn't wish to be

restored to her grandmother! After all, she is married to a Grand Duke of Russia.'

'But *I* wish her to be restored. The Empress will not refuse her, so much is certain—'

'And you will be rewarded.' Ogilvie leaned forward. 'Your Highness, I think there are matters of which I know nothing, and of which perhaps you have some knowledge. Among them is this: what do the Russians mean to achieve in Katmandu – and why do you wish them not to achieve it?'

The fat face closed up, retreating into its beard. 'I am a loyal subject, a ruler in the name of the Empress of India. That is enough for you, Captain Ogilvie. I ask you now to do your duty, which is to inform your Queen's loyal subject of the movement of your British Army, so that he may plan accordingly for the good of the British Raj...'

For the good of the British Raj... Ogilvie wondered, as he had wondered so often on Indian service, at the deviousness of the native mind that could utter the most blatant lies in the full expectation that they would be hailed as truth: self-deception was not the least of the Nawab's oily attributes!

198

The ruler had continued in his refusal to discuss his knowledge of any Russian aims; it was possible either that he knew nothing or that those aims were in fact of the purest innocence, a hypothesis that Ogilvie frankly found untenable in all the circumstances. It had been crystal clear, however, that the Nawab intended to play his very excellent hand for all it was worth; he had hinted wishfully at an extension of his lands, a large grant of money from the Calcutta government, and authority from the Viceroy to levy increased taxes on his own subjects. He was naturally under no illusion as to the great value of his hostage, whom he referred to punctiliously as his honoured guest; and equally naturally he was anxious not to lose her to a British expeditionary force before she had, as it were, paid for her keep. Loyal oiliness, Ogilvie felt as he paced the apartment he had been given, could go little further. Yet in fact it had gone a great deal further: Ogilvie pondered on what had been required of him. With politeness, with obsequious inclinations of the head whenever the name of the Queen-Empress had been spoken, with a soft tongue, the Nawab of Bandalpur had spelled it out amid much dialogue. Stripped of inessentials, it had come down to this: Ogilvie was to ride out of the city, a free man but alone, make for Peshawar along a route given him by the Nawab who would ensure that he came to no harm, and report that the Grand Duchess was safe in Bandalpur. This report was to be made personally to Lieutenant-General Fettleworth who was then to report only to the Viceroy in Calcutta, who would open diplomatic contacts with Bandalpur. The Grand Duchess would not be harmed in the meantime; but should Ogilvie exceed his order, or any British recovery force be sent out before an agreement had been reached in Calcutta, then Colour-Sergeant MacTrease and the surviving men of B Company would all be put to death. Once the agreement had been amicably reached, not only would the Nawab hand over the Grand Duchess to British military power outside his gates, but he would also make known to the Viceroy certain highly relevant and important details that had reached him from private sources in Kabul concerning the Russian mission to Nepal. Pondering all this now, Ogilvie looked down from the barred window of his opulent prison, down into a mud walled arena behind the palace. Earlier, the Nawab had shown him this arena, which was also overlooked by some of the windows of the ruler's council chamber below. The walls, which were high ones, closed in a sandy place with the look of a parade-ground, burning beneath the sun. They were ordinary enough but for one thing: the end of the wall was badly stained with a brownish substance.

'Blood,' the Nawab had said. 'Certain classes of criminals are put to death there.'

'How?'

'By stoning from the women, after emasculation. That is where your soldiers will see the last of our Indian sunlight, Captain Ogilvie. That is, if you do not do as I ask, or fail to do it successfully.'

'I see.' Ogilvie tried to keep emotion out of his voice, to be calm and controlled. 'You don't fear the power of the Empress of India, Your Highness – that her revenge would be swift, and terrible?'

'No. Swift and terrible it would be – I agree. If it came ... but it will not come, for the Grand Duchess will be in my hands until the agreement is concluded. As to afterwards ... The Empress does not retreat upon her word, Captain Ogilvie. I shall be secure. There are other factors also that ensure this.'

'And they are?'

The Nawab laughed. 'Why, the security of the Raj! Calcutta will be most highly anxious to know the Russians' intentions, and there will be no premature revenge that would set a body of British soldiers above the security of the Raj itself!'

In this, Ogilvie had recognised truth. Now, in his room, he turned away from the prospect of the mud wall, from a sudden searing vision of Highland blood upon it. He knew India well enough to know the intrigue that not even the British Raj could afford to stand aside from, knew that in moments of great decision a cold-blooded disregard for life could be accepted, even glossed over, in the infinitely greater interest. The one unshakeable rock was in fact the Queen-Empress herself, who would never countenance the expedient sacrifice of her soldiers; the same would apply to Lord Salisbury in Whitehall and to Lord Elgin and his staff in Calcutta; but there were imponderables to be dealt with, formidable obstacles. The civil servants of the great and powerful India Office took a more cold-blooded, clerkly view of common soldiers than did those with closer contact with the regiments of the British line; so did the mouthpieces of trade and commerce, the sordid money-makers out of India, the men who had their powerful lobbies, the men with the vested interests in the Raj and its continuance. Money talked loud; Ogilvie had no doubt that the Nawab's demands would be met. And, in fact, for them to be met would offer the one chance to his own men. Sick with dislike of an enforced decision, he crossed the apartment towards a brass gong hanging from a cedarwood frame upon an inlaid table. Taking up the stick, he beat twice upon the gong and the door opened. Flanked by two guards with drawn cavalry sabres, a servant bowed low.

'Yes, Sahib?'

'A message to His Highness. I am ready to ride.'

'The message will be delivered, Sahib.' Another bow: the man withdrew, the doors were shut and locked again.

'You say you are ready.'

Ogilvie nodded, he caught a glimpse of his reflection in a long mirror: he was, he felt, disgracing his uniform, his captain's stars and the tartan of the Royal Strathspey by agreeing to act as runner for the greasy, little Nawab of Bandalpur. 'I'm ready,' he said.

'But I am not. There is time yet.'

'For what?'

The Nawab said, smiling, 'For you to tell me what I asked, that is, the disposition of the British soldiers. It is known, of course, that there was a strong escort. Also I have heard rumours that another force of some strength will join the escort farther to the east, before the Nepal border – or would have done. Where are these forces now?'

'I don't know. Nor do I understand why you're so anxious to know.'

'Because, in spite of what I have said, I do not trust the British wholly. At times they are unpredictable.'

'You mean–'

'I mean,' the Nawab interrupted, pointing a finger at Ogilvie, 'that I shall not necessarily keep the Grand Duchess in the city. I have other places ... but before moving her, I must know it is safe to do so. Now do you understand, Captain Ogilvie?'

'Yes, I understand,' Ogilvie said, nodding. 'I'm sorry, though, I can't tell you.'

'You must know the orders.'

'I repeat, I'm sorry. I don't know them.'

'But I do not believe this. If you do not tell me, you will be most sorry, Captain Ogilvie!'

204

'Even if I did know,' Ogilvie said, 'I wouldn't be able to tell you. Taking your message is one thing, Your Highness, but no British officer can ever reveal his orders.'

The Nawab shrugged and pulled at his beard, thoughtfully, his eyes gleaming. 'I have said there is time. Time, it seems, is what you need, Captain Ogilvie, so you shall have it in plenty.' He turned for the door, and clapped his hands. The sabre-armed guards came into the apartment, backed this time by two more and commanded by a tall man who appeared to be an officer of the Nawab's army, a man full of years and soldierly-looking, a man with piercing dark eyes and a proud face: seeing this man, Ogilvie felt a sense of shock. The face was familiar; though he could give the man no name, he was convinced they had met before, and under very different circumstances. Moreover, he felt the recognition to be mutual and, in the case of the old native officer, to be accompanied by a strong degree of shame and embarrassment.

The Nawab, allowing no time for talk, indicated Ogilvie. 'Take him,' he said, licking his tongue around the full red lips. 'Take him to reflect, for he has much to think about!'

Much to think about indeed: notably about the native officer who escorted him. From his bearing a professional soldier, he had most likely once served the Raj: it would be within that context that Ogilvie would have encountered him. Ogilvie searched his memory as he was marched away, but vainly: time, perhaps, would help. He had anticipated being flung into some stinking dungeon, a place of rats and fleas and lice, and dank stench: instead he was marched out into the bright, high sunlight, into the mud-walled arena behind the palace. His helmet was removed and he was bound with strong cords to metal ring-bolts set into the wall. He was blindfolded: and, curiously, it was after the blindfold had been set in place that memory came back to him, crystal clear: the old soldier's name was Ayub Shaikh and he had indeed seen service with the Raj; their paths had cross some four years earlier. Moistening dry lips, he spoke as Ayub Shaikh's hands secured the cords of the blindfold.

'It is a long time, *Duffardar*-Major.'

There was a hiss of breath. 'A long time, Ogilvie Sahib.'

'Long enough, it seems, to change the

loyalties of the late *Duffardar*-Major of The Guides in his retirement?'

There was no answer: Ogilvie recalled the shame he had read earlier in Ayub Shaikh's face, recalled the circumstances of their last meeting. That had taken place during a routine patrol that had turned out to be anything but routine: Ogilvie's company had turned up in the nick of time when a squadron of The Guides had found themselves heavily outnumbered by a horde of bandits, their officers killed and the *Duffardar*-Major in command. Ayub Shaikh had sworn eternal friendship, making the infantry officer his brother in blood ... below the blindfold, Ogilvie gave a bitter smile: times changed, and men with them! Still giving no answer, Ayub Shaikh now told him to call out when he was ready to speak, ready to obey His Highness the Nawab; and then marched away with the escort. Ogilvie, alone now, could almost smell the dried blood, its sharp and sickly aroma brought out by the fierce sun. He could imagine the fall of jagged stones around the helpless victims who had died in this atrocious place, bleeding and in pain from the primitive and obscene surgery that had first been carried out on them. Fortunately the sun moved behind the lee of the palace walls before it had seriously affected him, though it left him with a blinding sick headache and a slight tremble in his limbs. Spared the worst of the sun, he was not spared a terrible ordeal during the early hours of the evening: there was no further need of imagination then. He heard the sounds first from far off, an increasing chatter of women that grew louder and became, as they approached, a high screaming. He felt the wind of something passing close, heard the soft thud as a flung missile hit the mud wall above his head, causing particles to drop over his head and face. More such thuds, then the first hit upon his right shoulder. It was a jagged stone, its sharp points biting into the khaki-drill tunic to draw blood. After that, they came thick and fast – not at his face and head but at his body: the Nawab, presumably, had no wish to risk killing his intended envoy. But his body suffered badly: chest, arms, knees, legs took the stones, and all the while the women's screaming was kept up, a horrible sound. No cloak of unconsciousness came to ease him: he could only hang in the cords and take all that came, humiliated, sick with burning anger that rose in his throat like bile and made him want to charge out and kill indiscriminately, lay about him with a claymore, women or not. These women were devils. At last, however, the stoning ceased. It ceased suddenly, and without any distinguishable command. One minute the air seemed full, then there was nothing. Hardly able to believe it was over, Ogilvie drooped against the binding cords, listening to the departing sounds, the excited but dwindling female chatter. Then he heard marching feet, a sound that approached and stopped close by. He felt the cords being cast off, felt men's hands take him in a strong grip and march him away. The blindfold was jerked off: he saw that the sun was well down into late evening. He was marched into the palace without a word of explanation, and taken down a flight of stone steps into an alleyway, also of stone, lit at intervals by smoking flares thrust into holders along the wall. The escort stopped by a door which their leader pushed open with a thrust of his foot.

Ogilvie was ordered in and the door was shut and heavily bolted behind him. At last, the dungeon. It was pitch dark, a total blackness in which he could see nothing at all. He moved cautiously behind outstretched hands: his finger-tips met cold stone. He followed it round, using his feet as carefully as his hands. The cell, he found, was square: he judged the walls to be no more than five or six feet in length. The floor was bare – no bed, no seat. And it was desperately stuffy, airless. The Black Hole of Calcutta without any fellow sufferers ... in here, if left for long, a man could suffocate. The cell had been cold upon his first arrival, but already his body-warmth was having its effect in creating a worse fug. He sat on the floor with his back against a wall: there was no point in movement. He sat in total silence, an unearthly silence as intense as the dark itself, waiting for the unknown. His mind was in a tumult: he could be behaving foolishly. Down here, he could be of no conceivable service to the Grand Duchess Sergius: all the same, a British officer did not reveal his orders or those of his superiors, nor the disposition of troops. On the other hand, there was no virtue in rigidity for its own sake, and if as a result the Queen's granddaughter should suffer, he was well in line to take the blame afterwards. One thing was sure: Bloody Francis Fettleworth would see to it that his own nose was kept demonstrably clean...

★ ★ ★

Ogilvie dropped into an uneasy sleep, a sleep of nightmares in which, once again, he endured the stoning of the native women and found himself, in the inexplicable weavings of nightmare, wandering among the grisly corpses of the cave back along the pass. He woke in a profuse cold sweat, and through the mists of a drug-like sleep heard his name called:

'Ogilvie Sahib!'

He stirred, but gave no answer: he saw that the door of his cell was open a little way, and there was light from the flares outside. The voice came again: 'Ogilvie Sahib, I come only to speak and to explain.' The narrow band of light widened, and a tall figure came in, leaving the door ajar behind him. Ogilvie felt a lurch in his heart, and came fully awake.

'*Duffardar*-Major?'

'Yes, Ogilvie Sahib. Ayub Shaikh, now Captain of His Highness's guard.'

Ogilvie raised himself on an elbow and stared at the face framed in yellow, guttering light. 'Once, we were brothers in blood, Ayub Shaikh.'

'I am sorry, Ogilvie Sahib.'

Harshly, Ogilvie laughed. 'Well may you be sorry for what you've done to an officer of the Raj ... to say nothing of the oath of friendship sworn at your own insistence, Ayub Shaikh. Is this how former soldiers of the Raj repay the Queen-Empress?'

'I am sorry, Ogilvie Sahib,' the old man said again, his voice humble and deeply moved. 'I have suffered no change in my loyalties, Ogilvie Sahib. I am loyal still to the Raj, and am now in the service of a prince also loyal to the Raj.'

'The Nawab?' Ogilvie was sardonic.

'Just so, Ogilvie Sahib—'

'Loyal principally, I think, to himself and his own aggrandisement. He's scarcely acting in the interest of the Raj at this moment, however much he may protest to the contrary.'

Ayub Shaikh inclined his head but did not comment. He went on, 'I am a soldier, and though old in years now, I cannot live without being a soldier. When I left the service of the Raj—'

'All right, Ayub Shaikh, that part at least I understand. Why have you come to me?'

'I come to ask forgiveness, Ogilvie Sahib.'

'Yet you would have stood by and watched me die if that had been necessary. Wouldn't you?'

There was a pause, then Ayub Shaikh said

212

in an unsteady voice, 'Sahib, I do not know. It did not happen. Yet I swore the oath of friendship, and I made you my brother in blood. I think I would have killed myself before my brother.' There was another pause. 'I have most distantly served under your honourable father, Ogilvie Sahib, as you know – the first time being when he was a Brigadier-General at Mardan. I was ashamed today at the stoning ... I have not words to say how great was my shame that it was I who had led you there at His Highness's command.'

Ogilvie nodded, his face dour. 'Shame,' he said evenly, 'is capable of descent to the next generation, and the next after that.'

'Sahib?'

'Memory returns in full, Ayub Shaikh. Four years ago you told me that your son was a *duffardar* in another squadron of The Guides, and that your son's son was a *sowar* hopeful of advancement.'

'Yes, Sahib–'

'They're still with the regiment?'

'They are, Sahib.'

'And have no wish to be drummed out, their buttons and badges hacked off by the cavalry sabres of their comrades?'

'Sahib!' There was a harshly drawn breath.

'You threaten this?'

'I do not threaten it, Ayub Shaikh. But it will happen – if British soldiers should die in Bandalpur, when your part becomes known, as it will – then the name of Ayub Shaikh will smell high to heaven in every cantonment in every military station of the British Raj.' He paused. 'Have a care for the honour of your descendants, Ayub Shaikh, before it is too late for shame to be extirpated!'

Ayub Shaikh, trembling all over now, asked in a low voice, 'You seek help from me, Ogilvie Sahib, in return for–'

'In return for help in escaping with my soldiers and with the Grand Duchess, I offer your son and grandson their honour.'

'Sahib, I cannot. It is impossible!'

Ogilvie shrugged. 'You must weigh it in the balance, and decide.' He found his body soaked with sweat: everything now depended on his personal powers of persuasion allied to a threat that any former *Duffardar-Major* would see as immense. It was no time to be mealy-mouthed, no time to allow considerations of soldierly decency to intrude between himself and his duty to the Raj. Shamelessly he reminded Ayub Shaikh of the power of the British Army, of the vast influence and authority of his own father, Commander-in-Chief in Murree, military representative in northern India of Her Majesty the Queen-Empress – whose own wrath would be boundless when her soldiers were known to have been imperilled by a former *Duffardar*-Major of her Indian Army. That *Duffardar*-Major would lose his status, would throw away all his years of honourable service ... Ogilvie laid it on thick, speaking in a low voice but firmly, with the whole confident authority of his upbringing and experience of India behind him, playing skilfully upon the old man's traditions of service and loyalty as well as upon the age-long regard in which the family unit was held, the absolute obligation never to dishonour. He knew exactly what he was asking: His Highness the Nawab of Bandalpur was possibly no worse and no better than any other Indian prince. Any one of them, in the circumstances, would condemn the Captain of his Guard to a terrible death afterwards. But Ogilvie stressed that Ayub Shaikh might well find himself his executioner, since he would never accede to the Nawab's demands; and further pointed out that Ayub Shaikh would do better to die honourably in the service of the Raj than to die by his own hand after killing his brother in blood. 'I believe you would die easier – and be more acceptable to your God! But you need not die, Ayub Shaikh. If you wish to return to British India, you shall come with me. With your help, I shall construct a plan. First I shall need to know the whereabouts of the Grand Duchess Sergius and of my soldiers. I'll want a ground plan of the palace. I'll need to know the beats and orders of the sentries, and the arrangements for the reliefs. Well, Ayub Shaikh?'

Aware of the rapid beating of his heart, he waited. Ayub Shaikh's head was in his hands and the old soldier's body was heaving, racked with deep sobs. Yet, when at last Ayub Shaikh lifted his head and looked into Ogilvie's eyes, Ogilvie knew before any word was spoken that he had persuaded well.

Chapter 12

'That patrol,' Fettleworth said, drumming his fingers on his desk top and staring at his Chief of Staff. 'The one I ordered out to find Margesson's brigade. Who was it, now?'

'The Duke of Cornwall's Light Infantry, sir–'

'Yes, yes. No result yet, I take it?'

'No, sir,' Brigadier-General Lakenham answered patiently. 'Had there been, you would have been the first to know.'

'Quite. I accept that. But there's been too much damn delay. I'm being pushed by Murree – by Sir Iain Ogilvie. I've had a personal letter, brought by the train, by hand of messenger.' Bloody Francis, scarlet in face and tunic, tapped his fingers on the crested writing paper of the despatch. *'He's* being pushed by Calcutta, and Lord Elgin has Whitehall on his back! I gather, without the precise words being said, that Her Majesty's been making a ... well, well, I'd better not be too precise, Lakenham, but I'm sure you understand. Damn it, the matter's urgent – vital! The Queen's granddaughter!'

'It's been well drummed in, sir.' Lakenham was patient still: the Divisional Commander was carrying much responsibility and was showing it. The portrait of Queen Victoria, staring Fettleworth in the face from the wall opposite his desk, was acting as a continual goad, and Bloody Francis always manifested a high degree of perturbation when under pressure ... Lakenham glanced up at the framed bun of hair, the lace widow's cap, the full black dress, the pursed lips. He met the stare of the eyes like a physical force, and looked away: too much pressure there, and not good for worried generals. 'Shall I order out another patrol, sir?'

'I don't know, damned if I do!' Fettleworth drummed away on his blotter. 'What d'you think – hey?'

Lakenham reflected. 'On balance I'd say not. Too many cooks, too many stray troops looking for each other in the hills – not a good thing. The Duke of Cornwall's will report in shortly, I've no doubt.'

'They could have been cut up, Lakenham.'

'That's always the risk, of course.'

Fettleworth fumed uncertainly. 'What the devil do I tell Murree?'

'I wouldn't tell them anything yet, sir. Hold on till we have news. India's full of delays!'

'That's all very well. I wish you'd show more concern, Lakenham. The one thing we just can't have now, is for that woman to cross into Nepal!' Bloody Francis tugged angrily at his flowing white moustache and bellowed for his bearer, demanding chota-pegs instantly.

'First the Grand Duchess,' Ogilvie said, 'then we'll make contact with my soldiers. You can bring the Grand Duchess to me?'

'Yes, Ogilvie Sahib. Come with me now, and keep very quiet.'

Ogilvie had no need of the warning. Behind Ayub Shaikh, he moved fast but silently along the passage outside the cell, beneath the light of the flares. At the end of the passage Ayub Shaikh, fully committed now, led the way past the stone steps down which Ogilvie had come earlier, heading for a heavy door beyond. This he unlocked, but did not open. 'Remain here, Ogilvie Sahib,' he said. 'Inside the passage. When I return, it will be with the Grand Duchess. I shall bring her to the outside, and knock on the door three times, then once, before opening the door. You understand, Sahib?'

Ogilvie nodded. 'Off you go, Ayub Shaikh, and make it fast.'

The old soldier turned away, climbing the stone steps to the ground floor of the palace above. Ogilvie waited in considerable tension. Ayub Shaikh had discounted the likelihood of anyone coming down in his absence, but Ogilvie was ready with strong hands and arms if they should do so, ready to squeeze the breath from any native body. That wait seemed endless, racking Ogilvie with thoughts of possible last-minute treachery. His relief was immense when at last he heard the knocks on the great door, and it swung open, creaking a little on ancient rusty hinges, to reveal Ayub Shaikh and the Grand Duchess – silhouetted, by an unkind Providence, in bright moonlight. Not giving the Grand Duchess a chance to speak, Ayub Shaikh beckoned Ogilvie out.

'Keep very close against the palace wall, Ogilvie Sahib,' he said in a whisper. 'On this side of the palace we should not be seen, but care is necessary even so. No noise, please. Follow me.'

He turned away. Following, a hand on the

arm of the Grand Duchess, Ogilvie glanced briefly at her face in the moonlight. In all truth she was little more than a girl in looks, though in her early thirties by age. A trusting face and an open one, long shaped and with a patrician nose – more reminiscent of portraits of the Prince Consort than of the Queen, Ogilvie thought. A pretty woman, and one with obvious spirit. She had met his glance, giving him a rather shy smile, but a brave one. Her head was high and her back straight. The Princess Elizabeth Fedorovna was no wilting lily, no hothouse flower of palace life, and Ogilvie, too well aware of present dangers, was much relieved to see it. They went on behind Ayub Shaikh, making for the corner of the palace wall which seemed to tower into the moonlit sky like some castle from a fairy story dwarfed only by a hard jagged outline of the mountain crests beyond. Coming up to an abutment, Ayub Shaikh held up a hand for them to stop. He pointed ahead. 'Over there to the left, Ogilvie Sahib, are the stables.'

Ogilvie nodded. Above the stables, Ayub Shaikh had told him, was the barrack-room of the Nawab's soldiers; behind the stables was a guardroom in which the men of the 114th Highlanders were being held. 'We're well away from the palace gate, I take it?'

'Yes, Sahib. If we are careful, nothing will be heard at the gate.'

'Right!' Ogilvie took a long look across the ground towards the stable area. 'We'll go ahead now, Ayub Shaikh.' He turned to the Grand Duchess. 'Ma'am, I must ask you to remain here, and keep hidden behind the abutment.' He hesitated. 'I think Ayub Shaikh will have told you what we're going to do in the next few minutes. It's risky. Are you still willing to take the chance?'

'Very willing,' she said, smiling. 'But cannot I take some active part in helping you both, Captain Ogilvie?'

'I'm sorry, Ma'am. According to Ayub Shaikh, for a woman to cross the courtyard at this hour – if seen, it would be thought unusual.'

The Grand Duchess nodded. 'I'm in your hands,' she said, 'and will do precisely as I'm told.' She laid the tips of her fingers, impulsively, on an arm of each of them. 'You're brave men and I'm deeply, deeply grateful.'

They crossed the empty space beneath the moon, openly and not too fast, with Ogilvie ahead of Ayub Shaikh whose revolver was held ostentatiously towards his back. There was no movement other than their own, no-one to see beyond a solitary sentry who, when Ayub Shaikh's footsteps were heard approaching, emerged from a cubby-hole by the stables and saluted his officer.

'Is all well, Siddiq Ali?' Ayub Shaikh asked.

'All is well, Sahib.'

Ahead of Ayub Shaikh, Ogilvie moved closer: he did his work quickly and efficiently. Using the heavy barrel of a revolver provided by Ayub Shaikh, he struck hard at Siddiq Ali's head. Without a sound the sentry slid into his arms and he dragged the limp body into cover. Then he followed Ayub Shaikh towards the stables, from which came the restless sounds of the horses in their stalls, the movement of hooves, the creak of leather. Otherwise, silence. Ayub Shaikh indicated a stairway leading upwards. 'The barrack-room,' he whispered. 'Come and we shall gather arms and uniforms.'

He led the way up the stairs, taking immense care, moving as stealthily as a cat. Behind him, Ogilvie reached a landing. Ayub Shaikh, his mouth close to Ogilvie's ear, whispered again and pointed. 'The sleeping quarters there. The armoury here. Come.' He moved for the armoury, very quietly opened the door. The room was filled with the moonlight striking off the racked jezails along the walls. The uniforms on their hangers stood out, splendid and colourful, down the centre. Quickly Ogilvie pulled on one of these gaudy liveries. Ayub Shaikh pointed to a machine-gun, a Maxim, in a corner of the room. 'A piece as used by the British Army, as you will recognise,' he said. 'Well cleaned and oiled.'

'I'll use that to cover the barrack-room,' Ogilvie said. 'Give me a hand to set it up.'

Together, and in silence, they lifted the Maxim and carried it out to the landing, setting it up on its tripod outside the barrack-room. 'Now my soldiers,' Ogilvie whispered. 'You have ten minutes, Ayub Shaikh. Use them well.' As catlike as before, Ayub Shaikh went back down the stairs. Occasionally snores came from the barrack-room. The minutes dragged past. Sounds came up to Ogilvie from below, the movement of men, kept to a minimum but nevertheless rasping at his nerves. Then more sound, the noise of horses moving out of the stables, noise that could not fail to waken the sleeping native soldiers in the barrack-room. Ogilvie sweated, waited with the Maxim's muzzled aimed squarely through the entry. Looking into the barrack-room, Ogilvie saw men stirring, sitting up in the bunks, exchanging glances: two of them came towards the landing, saw the Maxim and Ogilvie behind it.

'Go back and remain quiet,' Ogilvie said in Pushtu. 'If there is a sound, not a man will live.'

The two natives moved back fast: there was excited chatter, kept low. From the stables came further noise, the backing and filling of the horses as they were led out, the rattle and creak of the stairs: relays of Scots to carry down armfuls of native uniforms. Then, later, Colour-Sergeant MacTrease, with the whispered word that the Royal Strathspeys were mustered and mounted and that a horse was ready for the officer.

'The wounded, Colour MacTrease?'

'All correct, sir. Those not fit to ride alone are held on their horses by the men on either side. Will you come down now, sir?'

Ogilvie nodded. 'Give me a hand with the Maxim.'

'Sir?'

'We'll take it with us, down the stairs.' He raised his voice towards the barrack-room, speaking once again in Pushtu. 'If you wish to live, you will remain where you are, and in silence still. The stairway will be covered from below by the Maxim gun.' He gestured at MacTrease; together they lifted the heavy gun and backed towards the stairs. No one emerged in pursuit. They jammed the mechanism of the Maxim and ran for the waiting horses. Mounted, Ogilvie turned and glanced briefly down the line of horsemen, his Highlanders in their strange native uniforms, with the Grand Duchess, also accoutred as a Nawab's man, in the centre. It was touch and go still: the native troopers in the barrack-room would clearly not remain static for much longer, but thus far the plan held. Facing front again, Ogilvie passed the order to move out for the palace gates. With Ayub Shaikh impassive-faced in the lead, they broke into a canter, bearing down upon the gate guard in strength. Ayub Shaikh, a commanding figure on horseback, shouted at the sentries to open up. His heart in his mouth Ogilvie, even now not wholly certain that the Captain of the Guard would not change his mind at the last and regain his position with the Nawab, watched the great iron-bound wooden gates swing open. The horses were pulled up, impatiently waiting; the moment the gap was wide enough, Ayub Shaikh rode ahead, lifting a hand for the general advance, and they followed through. Ogilvie let out a long breath of relief, but knew they were far from safe yet. They rode at a fast pace through the narrow, filthy streets of the city, watched by curious faces that began to peer from windows as the clatter of soldiery was heard. At this hour the alleys themselves were empty; there were no hindrances and no time was lost, nor, as yet, was there any sound of pursuit from the palace. Hopes rose: MacTrease was grinning, and a private was starting to bawl out the words of a Scots song.

'Quiet!' Ogilvie snapped. 'You're a native, Private Thomas – remember?'

'I'm sorry, sir.' The man sang no more. Out of the last of the smelly alleys of the town, they stormed across the open space before the city gates. Again Ayub Shaikh shouted ahead for free passage out, once again the gates were opened for them. They passed through in safety, scarcely able to believe their luck. Turning in the saddle as they went ahead across the plain at the gallop, Ogilvie saw the gates being shut behind them.

The main body of the brigade column under Brigadier-General Margesson was now halted on the west bank of the Jhelum River, which Margesson had decided he would not cross just yet. Although the official reason was to rest the men and horse, there was in fact a degree of paralysing indecision at Brigade. All the officers knew that the Brigadier-General was playing with fire and was about to get his fingers badly burned: the facts of the disappearance of the Grand Duchess should have been reported some days since to Division, where by now the utmost confusion must be prevailing in the military mind of General Fettleworth.

Lord Dornoch did his best in his acting capacity as Chief of Staff.

'I'd suggest, sir,' he said as the column was fallen out on the river bank, 'that you send back a detail to Division at this stage.'

Margesson shook his head. 'I'm not giving in, Dornoch.'

'I'd not see it in that light, sir.'

'Wouldn't you?' Margesson studied Dornoch over the bowl of his pipe as he lit it. 'Would *you* hand yourself to General Fettleworth on a plate?'

228

Dornoch sighed. He had come to have a regard for Margesson as a man – he was no hanger back when it came to action, and he dealt fairly with the men; but there was no virtue nor good sense in self-deception, and Dornoch was convinced that the Brigadier-General was blinding himself to the realities of a worsening situation. Indeed, it was almost criminal obstinacy that he had not at once sent back a report to Peshawar upon the disappearance of the Grand Duchess – in Dornoch's view, an inconceivable error of judgement. True he would have incurred the intensest displeasure of all higher authority from the Queen downward, but he would have been able to offer a defence upon his subsequent return to cantonments. Now, in hugging his failure to himself in the hope of turning it into success meanwhile, Margesson was risking his whole career and more importantly, the very life of the Grand Duchess. Dornoch could not avoid feeling some personal responsibility: in the beginning he had perhaps been less insistent than common sense demanded. Time had crept up on them all: immediately after the disappearance of the Russians, immediately after the Countess Denarov had rejoined the column, it had appeared reasonable to await the results of a search before reporting back. Since then, there had been drift into a kind of point of no return.

Dornoch tried diplomatically to get all this into the Brigade Commander's head; but without success.

'No, no, Dornoch, it's still up to me. We have the patrols out.' This was true enough: Margesson had, after much argument, at least sanctioned the detailing of patrols of half-company strength to scour the surrounding hills – so far with an intensely worrying lack of any success. 'We must wait, that's all. Wait.'

'But Division has more resources–'

'Yes, we all know that!' Margesson spoke tetchily: his nerves were clearly giving him little peace. 'I've said before, Fettleworth will initiate a bloody war right through the Frontier provinces and still won't have any more success than we. It's our load, Dornoch – or mine anyway! I have to carry it.' He puffed clouds of smoke from his pipe, eyes narrowed in concentration as he held the match. 'The orders stand, Colonel.' He looked up suddenly. 'How's Count Tomislav?'

Dornoch smiled. 'Colour Burnett is a good drill-sergeant and a hard taskmaster!

The Count is tired.'

A spark of humour appeared in Margesson's eye. 'And hungry?'

'Very, I shouldn't wonder.'

'Well, I'm tired too, if not hungry, but it can't be helped. Bring him along, if you please, Dornoch, and we'll have another go at him.'

Dornoch, turning to beckon up a runner, changed his mind. Prisoner under escort or not, Count Tomislav was still a Colonel of Cossacks. Dornoch rode down the column himself to where the Russian was sitting in the dust beside the track, with his armed escort taking their ease beside him. At Dornoch's approach the soldiers sprang to attention. Telling them to sit down again, Dornoch called Count Tomislav aside.

'The General's compliments, Count Tomislav. He wishes to speak to you.'

'I do not wish to speak to him, Colonel. I spit on him.' Graphically, a stream of saliva landed at the feet of Dornoch's horse. 'I have nothing to tell him, nothing.'

'Nevertheless, you'll attend upon Brigade as ordered. Come – there will be no escort other than myself, unless you refuse, in which case you'll be dragged. The choice is yours entirely.'

Count Tomislav bared his long yellow teeth in a savage grimace, but decided to make the best of it. He turned and stalked towards Brigade, moving ahead of Lord Dornoch's horse, holding himself erect, boldly. When he reached the Brigadier-General's presence, Margesson's luncheon table was being prepared. Tomislav's eyes gleamed with hunger even though no food had arrived as yet: the white cloth, the cutlery and silver were enough to stir the imagination of any hungry man. His mouth watering, Tomislav was seeing in his mind's eye good meat and fish, and wine, and perhaps ripe English cheese ... he met Margesson's sardonic look, and glowered. He would say nothing; he would never betray his Czar. He countered all Margesson's questions with stonewall silence, watching, eventually, Margesson eat a hearty meal in the company of munching staff officers.

Chapter 13

They were not left long in peace, as was inevitable: the pursuit was heard in the thunder of horses' hooves when Ogilvie's cavalcade had galloped a matter of some five miles from the gates of Bandalpur. The moon showed the native cavalry streaming across the plain.

Ogilvie called to MacTrease: 'Two squadrons, Colour MacTrease. Ranks to detach to right and left and re-form. I'll take the right, and you the left. The men carrying the wounded to ride clear and keep at a safe distance.'

'Aye, sir! And the lady?'

'She'll detach with the wounded detail. Carry on, Colour MacTrease.'

The orders were shouted: MacTrease understood what the manoeuvre was likely to be, though the next action depended upon the pursuers. Either they would execute a similar movement and split their forces, or they would ride on in formation. If they chose the latter course, the Royal Strathspeys, riding out to the flanks initially, would close in again and attack from both sides simultaneously. It was fifty-fifty and could not be forecast. Ogilvie, riding out hard with his half of the squadron, Ayub Shaikh by his side, found himself praying that the enemy would take the second choice. Reaching his limit of flanking movement, Ogilvie ordered the turn and then the half, and waited with his squadron facing towards the native cavalry. He saw the column of horsemen, surprisingly, also come to the halt, still in close formation. Taking his chances, he raised a hand and shouted loudly across the plain to MacTrease. Both half-squadrons got on the move together, charging at full gallop down on the halted native line to the accompaniment of wild Highland war-cries. As the British hoofbeats thundered down, the native cavalry seemed to falter, some of the riders making off to the rear, others charging ahead, some swaying out sideways. A ragged fire came from them, but the Royal Strathspeys rode on hell for leather, bearing down on both flanks of the disintegrating pursuit, waiting Ogilvie's order to open fire.

When that order came, the result was even more ragged than the fire of the enemy: the Scots were too inexperienced to handle the jezails well from the backs of pounding horses. But the weight of the combined charge told truly: the Scots threw themselves down upon the natives, yelling still, and once in amongst them began the hand-to-hand fighting with the cold steel of bayonets. Cries of agony ripped into the night: there was vengefulness in the manner of the bayonet-thrusts, a sheerly murderous intent to teach the natives that Scots could not be trifled with. Men and horses went down in the wildest confusion, and as the Highlanders steadied on their horses the jezails came into their own. Bullets and club-swung butts joined the bayonets, and the remnant of the native force broke to the rear, riding off into the night and leaving many dead and wounded behind. Ogilvie, glancing sideways, saw Ayub Shaikh still at his side.

'You fought with us, Ayub Shaikh,' he said, and smiled. 'You have no regrets?'

'None, Sahib. My trust now is in the Raj and the Queen-Empress.'

Ogilvie held out his hand: Ayub Shaikh took it in a strong grip. Ogilvie said, 'It'll not be misplaced, I promise.' He hesitated, frowning. 'Tell me now, *Duffardar*-Major ... have you any knowledge of what His Highness the Nawab was after, in regard to the Grand Duchess ... any helpful words as to what's afoot?'

Ayub Shaikh gave a shrug. 'None, Sahib. I am but a soldier. And yet...'

'Go on, Ayub Shaikh.'

There was another shrug. 'It is only conjecture ... but I have overheard talk that gives substance ... and I have heard crying from the apartment of Her Imperial Highness. I believe she has no wish to go forward into Nepal.'

'Anything else?'

'I believe danger awaits her there, Ogilvie Sahib. I do not know what form this danger may take. Indeed I know nothing more. Had I such knowledge, I would tell you.'

'I accept that, Ayub Shaikh.' Ogilvie turned away to seek out the Grand Duchess. He found her unhurt and with an escort of Scots around her horse. She was pale in the moon's light, but composed.

'I'm sorry you had to see that, Ma'am,' Ogilvie said breathlessly as he saluted.

'No apologies, please, Captain Ogilvie,' she said in a shaking voice. Ogilvie saluted again, and pulled his horse round, calling out to MacTrease to have the new British wounded lifted onto the saddles to join the others. As soon as this had been done, he gave the order to ride out: no delay could be accepted now, the native wounded had to be left for their own people to bring in. In formation again, the Scots galloped off towards the peaks to the south, reaching the cover of the foothills without further trouble. As dawn came up the sky they rode deep into the passes, not yet stopping to rest men and horses.

'From now on, Ogilvie Sahib,' Ayub Shaikh said sombrely, 'we shall be hunted men.'

Ogilvie grinned. 'From here to eternity!'

'Sahib?'

'Never mind. We'll not think about eternity just yet! We'll head for something more of this world, Ayub Shaikh – my brigade, which should be somewhere south and east of us. In the meantime, a word with Her Royal Highness might be of use.'

First the wounded had to be attended to so far as was possible – those hurt in the recent action, and those from the battle before the ride to Bandalpur. The latter had received some attention whilst confined in the palace, and most of them were in not too bad a shape. Surgery, primitive enough but effective, had removed bullets from arms and fleshy parts, and bayonet wounds had been bandaged. After full daybreak Ogilvie called a halt by a clear mountain stream, and while the horses were rested he removed the bandages with MacTrease's assistance and had them washed out in the water and hung to dry in the sun. Articles of clothing were torn up and similarly washed and dried for use as bandages for the freshly wounded men. The water-bottles were refilled, but there was no food: on that score alone, it was vital they should find Margesson's column without delay.

The Grand Duchess assisted, at her own desire, with the rudimentary medical attentions, bringing comfort to the men simply by talking to them and using a woman's presence to give them heart. While she busied herself with the blood-caked dressings, Ogilvie watched her: she was full of calmness and serenity, seeming to care little for her own discomfort and danger. Ogilvie found it hard to tie her in now with the weeping that Lord Dornoch had heard coming from the closed palanquin whilst on the march with the Cossacks. Waiting, a little later, for the bandages and torn-up clothing to dry out, he took the Grand Duchess aside.

Formally he said, 'Ma'am, my apologies, but it's necessary I ask you some questions now.'

She smiled attractively, putting him at his ease by sitting down on a rock surface and bidding him sit also. She said, 'Naturally, Captain Ogilvie, I expected you to do so.' She paused, 'I understand your father is Sir Iain Ogilvie?'

'Yes, Ma'am—'

'You're very like him,' she said. 'I met him once, when I was staying at Balmoral with Grandmama.' There was a faraway look in her shadowed eyes. 'Such wonderful holidays in those days, with my English relations. I spent a good deal of time in England as well as Scotland. Buckingham Palace, Windsor ... I loved the green of England in the summer. Do you not miss it, out here in India?'

Ogilvie nodded. 'At times, very much, though in my case it's Scotland rather than England.'

'You know Deeside?'

'I do, Ma'am. Our own recruiting area –

and my home – is to the north and west of it ... not so far off.' He looked around the peaks, the jags of rock and the brown slopes of the hills harsh beneath the mounting sun. 'The lack of summer green apart, it's not so different from all this!'

'But safer.'

He laughed. 'Safer, yes! No sudden bullets–'

'Which may come at any time, Captain Ogilvie?'

'I have pickets out, Ma'am. You're well protected.'

'I know that,' she said quickly, then asked, 'Where do you propose to take me now, Captain Ogilvie?'

He told her that his objective was the main column heading east for Nepal. 'But whether or not you enter Nepal, Ma'am ... I think that has yet to be decided. If I may, I'll be frank. General Margesson was worried ... he was surprised that you didn't wish to meet him. Since then, I've learned that you may be in some danger, if you should cross into Nepal.'

'And it's that,' she said in a low voice, 'that you are going to question me about! Am I right, Captain Ogilvie?'

'Quite right, Ma'am. My duty–'

'Yes, I know – I understand.'

'Of course, if you wish to speak to General Margesson rather than me, Ma'am, that would be natural and perfectly proper. But we're certainly a long way from the column yet, and–'

'And in the meantime, anything may happen?'

'Yes.'

'Therefore you should know the facts – just in case I should be snatched away again–'

'Ma'am, I–'

'No, no, Captain Ogilvie, I'm not a child. I'm not afraid to face the possibilities. In my country – my country of Russia, I mean – life has taught me that if nothing else!' A shudder ran through her body; for a while she sat in silence, and Ogilvie didn't break into her thoughts. Then she said quietly, 'Very well, you shall be told. It is simple enough! My brother-in-law, Czar Nicholas, wishes to make a treaty with the King of Nepal. It's to be a trading treaty so far as the rest of the world is concerned, but there are to be other aspects–'

'Military aspects?'

'Yes. In brief, Captain Ogilvie, a military alliance between Russia and Nepal, directed

241

against the British Raj. There will also be an agreement with Kabul ... the result, as you can see, being that the northern part of India will be in a pincer grip between Nepal, Afghanistan and Russia when the time comes.'

'Is it coming, Ma'am?'

She shook her head sadly. 'I don't know, Captain Ogilvie. I know of no plans, but military alliances aren't usually made without some positive intent behind them, are they? One thing at least is certain, and that is when the time does come, then it will be Russian soldiers and Russian money that will make it all possible.'

'And you, Ma'am?'

'I?' The Grand Duchess smiled with immense sadness. 'I am torn in half. By birth I am German, yet half of me is English... and I have those happy memories of Grandmama and her court. You understand?'

'Of course I do. Then there is your new country–'

'Yes. My country is now Russia – my husband's country. I love my husband, Captain Ogilvie, very deeply. I respect him, and detest the wicked things that are said about him, which are all untrue – but such things you will not know about, of course, and do not need to.' She looked away from him, scuffing a foot in the dust of the track. 'Whichever way I turn I have to be at least half a traitor, yet my loyalty has to be to my husband's country in the first place. I cannot let him down – he has so many enemies, and his position as Governor-General of Moscow is precarious, even his life may be. He objected to my being sent, but was over-ruled by the Czar.' She was silent for a while, seeming to stiffen an inner resolve. 'I must cross into Nepal, Captain Ogilvie, I must!'

'But you don't want to?' Ogilvie said, remembering what Ayub Shaikh had told him.

'There is nothing,' she said bitterly, 'that I *want* less!'

'Because of your English connections, Ma'am?'

She nodded. Ogilvie asked, 'Ma'am, may I beg you to be precise as to your own part in the treaty negotiations? Also Count Tomislav's?'

She said, 'Oh, Count Tomislav is a simple soldier, nothing more–'

'An escort, and – a gaoler?'

She looked at him sharply, and coloured; but she said, 'Yes, a gaoler if you like. As for me, I'm to be the negotiator. Because of his hold over my husband the Grand Duke, Czar Nicholas knows I shall not fail.' Suddenly she put her head in her hands, and her shoulders shook. Ogilvie, embarrassed beyond words, watched her tears for a moment, then left her alone.

They moved out, continuing towards the east: gradually the track dipped a little south. Ogilvie, mapless now for he had been stripped of his equipment in Bandalpur, led the small force from his own knowledge alone. He believed they were not far off the Jhelum River, but whether or not they would strike the river in a fordable spot was in the lap of the gods. In the meantime the passes stood empty; there was no sign of any extended scouts from Margesson's column which, if it was in the vicinity, must surely be sending out parties to watch for Ogilvie's detached company. In point of fact, the column could be almost anywhere: Margesson could have decided to turn back for Peshawar after an interval of waiting, so as to alert Division for a full-scale search operation. More likely, though, he would have remained as an advanced force and sent back runners with his report ... and if this was the case, then he could surely not be all that far off? Worried and uncertain, Ogilvie held to his own earlier decision to ride on in the hopes of making contact, seeing no other course open to him now: to attempt to reach Peshawar would bring them back much too close to the domains of Bandalpur...

So far at any rate, they rode unmolested, and the farther they rode eastward the less became the chance of any attack inspired directly by the Nawab. Ogilvie, puzzling as to the lack of Pathan marauders, came to the conclusion that the Nawab was unwilling to extend his machinations too far from his palace: somewhere around was a British force, and it no doubt behoved His Highness, rather than to fight the British in the open field, to repair his broken fences! Having failed, the more important objective might well become reinstatement in the good books of the Raj. Ogilvie found his ponderings on the Grand Duchess to be more worrying for the future, though these worries were more for Brigadier-General Margesson than for him. What the devil, he wondered, were they to do about her? The answer was fairly obvious, of course: ride her back when in Brigade strength again, to Peshawar. There were now no Cossacks to fight if that were done, thanks to the Nawab of Bandalpur – except presumably Count Tomislav himself, still evading the clutches of the Nawab! But what would happen to the Grand Duchess when she returned in humiliation to St Petersburg? She was a brave woman, and Ogilvie was immensely sorry, the more so as she appeared now to have thrown herself slap onto his mercies and his conscience and his own loyalties. One thing had become clear enough: Count Tomislav had been perfectly right when he had told the Brigadier-General that Her Imperial Highness had no wish to have any British officers presented: her shame would have been too great.

Ogilvie, pondering the terrible pressures of Court life, with all the ramifications of family beyond the frontiers, was glad enough to be a commoner and a soldier. If in this world one was royalty, it seemed one could not escape mental agony sooner or later: there was scarcely anyone of the royal blood who was not bound in the imperial chain of consanguinity by Queen Victoria's avid marriage-bureaucracy.

'Sar'nt-Major!'
'Sir!' Cunningham turned upon being

called sharply, and slammed a salute at Andrew Black.

'The men are slack, Mr Cunningham.'

'Sir–'

'And slovenly! I will not have it.' Black streamed sweat, his trews sticking heavily to spindly thighs. 'You will kindly wake up their ideas, Sar'nt-Major. I don't like to see men lying around with too little to do.'

Cunningham's moustache twitched with anger. 'With respect, Captain Black, sir, the men are not at fault in having too little to do. They're bored with the inactivity, sir.'

'They are, are they?'

'Yes, sir.'

'I see. I understand! Then they will be provided with matters to occupy their minds and bodies, Sar'nt-Major. Those not detailed as pickets or for the advanced scouting parties during the rest of the day, will parade in fifteen minutes' time–'

'*Parade*, sir? Parade, out here in the hills?'

'You heard what I said, Sar'nt-Major. The Royal Strathspeys will parade with the pipes and drums, and put more heart into the whole column thereby. Inform Pipe-Major Ross, if you please.'

Cunningham breathed hard, his face frosty; but he saluted and walked away to

247

pass the orders, his back rigid, his pace-stick held almost quivering beneath his arm. Never in all his service had he been given such an order: a pound to a penny the Colonel would go up in smoke! Cunningham lifted his voice to the colour-sergeants, drill-sergeants and corporals and sent a runner to the Pipe-Major in his bivouac. Oaths filled the air: fists were shaken behind the back of the Brigade Major as he strode away down the resting lines. Resentfully, the Scots fell in by companies, companies depleted by the various duty requirements of temporary encampment and detached search parties. To the right of the battalion line, the pipes and drums mustered, the streamers drooping limply from the drones in the windless air, the high sun bringing up the dark colours of the Highland kilts.

Andrew Black returned, sweeping his glance over the assembled, hostile battalion. One by one the company commanders reported, saluting smartly. 'March and counter-march within battalion limits,' Black ordered, standing rigidly at attention. 'The turn will be made at the one end at Brigade, the other end at the lines of the Border Regiment.' His chest swelled. 'Battalion, slope ... *arms*! The Royal Strathspeys will advance in column of fours to the right! Battalion, right ... turn! By the right, quick ... march!'

Arms swung and sloped rifles were held steady as disgruntled men marched off. Air was puffed into the pipes as the drumbeats started and a moment later the music swelled out strong, vibrant. "The Old 93rd" echoed savagely back from the nearer hills; instinctively the Scots' shoulders straightened, the arms swung more vigorously. At the extremity of the battalion line, Pipe-Major Ross lifted his staff high in the air and led the pipes and drums in their turn-about to counter-march back right through the rank and file who followed on in their turn. All along the bivouacs, men stood up from the other regiments to watch and listen. At Brigade, Margesson also stood, looking down the line with a hand raised to shield his eyes from the sun. He turned to Lord Dornoch.

'A smart turn-out,' he said.

'Thank you, sir.'

'A good idea on Black's part. Stirs the spirit! The English regiments like to see it, I believe!'

'And we Scots like our music to be heard – especially by the English!' Dornoch smiled.

'Yes, it was a good idea, though I doubt if it was seen as such by the men in the first instance!' They stood together for a while, listening to the sounds rising and falling as the pipes and drums came and went. Nostalgic and haunting though they were, and often immensely sad and somehow lonely, the pipes of Scotland always had an unquenchable ring of triumph and victory, as though to wherever they brought a touch of the Highland spirit, success was bound to follow. Dornoch sent out a long, long breath. Black had indeed done the right thing, if possibly accidentally and with different intent: at least for a space, despondent men rallied.

They were tired now, lolling on the backs of the horses as the animals, equally tired, plodded on along the pass: worse than tiredness was the hunger. The few berries and other eatables they had found along the way had not been enough to help hollow stomachs and the resulting discomfort that would soon become the agony of distension. The Grand Duchess had been suffering with the rest, her cheeks drawn and pale as she rode her horse along between rocks and loose stones, through the dust and the heat that had cooled into evening and a cold bivouac in such shelter as could be found. They had made a start again with the dawn, mounting with a terrible hopelessness brought on by the empty stomachs. So far water was no real problem, though as a measure of simple prudence for an uncertain future it was rationed out twice daily by Colour-Sergeant MacTrease, with an extra issue for the wounded men whenever it became essential. The wounded were suffering badly now: two had died, falling belated victims to unhygienic native surgery's poisonous after-effects: the committal to the rock hard ground had taxed the strength of the burial party to the limit. Ogilvie and MacTrease had helped personally, taking the places of men who had dropped out, sick and shaking with fatigue. The ride had been resumed with an effort, the men staring dull-eyed into a hopeless prospect of slow starvation, though Ogilvie felt strongly that the direction was the right one, the decision good yet, that they could not now be far off the Jhelum River where more food should grow, and where perhaps they could rest awhile to restore their strength and purpose. Fighting hard to keep his mind alert and his eyelids open, he forced the men to push on, using words of encouragement and sometimes words of harsh anger that brought insubordinate retorts to which he turned deaf ears. They moved on and on, beneath the sun's cruel heat, beneath the black flap of waiting vultures' wings, listening to the occasional squawking cry from the death birds, the scavengers, the bone-cleaners with blood on their beaks. On and on, and later other sounds came to them from the distance, at first meaningless to weary brains but after a while beginning to assume a rhythm, a pattern ... a well-known one. Ogilvie gave his head a shake: a mental mirage, no more?

The sounds continued: Ogilvie felt a surge of spirit and turned to his colour-sergeant. 'D'you hear that, MacTrease? *Do you hear it, man?*'

'Hear what, sir?' MacTrease drooped on his horse, almost around its neck. 'I hear yon bloody carrion birds, that's all I hear.'

'It's more than that!' Ogilvie turned in the saddle, his eyes alight, looking back at his weary Scots with hope and bounding relief in his face. 'Ride at attention now, remember who you are! Straighten up there, d'you hear?' His voice rose. 'It's the pipes and drums ... we're closing the column!'

Chapter 14

Coming round a spit of rock with the Jhelum River now in thankful view, Ogilvie saw the long British column below, with the 114th Highlanders marching to the skirl of the pipes and the drummers' beat. His heart full, he lifted a hand for his company to follow, and rode ahead. In the moment of sheer relief at finding his regiment, he forgot that he must give the appearance of an advancing enemy: this solemn fact was borne in upon him when he heard a shout, followed by the crack of a rifle from behind a scrubby bush halfway up the hillside where a picket lay concealed.

'Hold your fire!' Ogilvie shouted at the top of his voice as, below, the pipes and drums suddenly stopped playing. The head of the picket appeared over the top of the bush, a puzzled look in the face. There seemed to be efficiency, however misplaced on this occasion, at Brigade: Ogilvie heard the notes of

Margesson's bugler, an alarm to arms quickly taken up along the column and saw Andrew Black riding fast towards the van. Ogilvie shouted to his company to dismount and get into cover: just in time, they did so. As they went flat on their stomachs, a heavy concentration of rifle and Maxim fire swept the hillside and Ogilvie felt the wind of the bullets zipping over his head. He swore savagely: he felt MacTrease's hand on his shoulder.

'The picket heard, sir. Look!'

Ogilvie looked: the picket, a lance-corporal from one of the English battalions, was on his feet and racing down into the low ground by the river. From cover, they watched, and saw the man double up to Andrew Black. Black stared towards the hills, shielding his eyes with a hand, then rode fast for Brigade. A few moments later the bugles sounded again, and the blazing rifles fell silent.

Ogilvie got to his feet and ordered his company to remount. They rode down the slope carefully, with a mind for the wounded men, and met a curious silence and the stares of many hundreds of eyes. As they neared the column Andrew Black rode forward, his face dark, his eyes watchful, his revolver ready in his hand.

'Who goes there?'

'Friend, Andrew,' Ogilvie called back.

'By God,' Black said. 'It's you, Captain Ogilvie!'

'Correct, Captain Black. With the Grand Duchess Sergius.'

Ogilvie rode forward. As he and his men rejoined the column there was a burst of cheering and shouting and helmets were thrown high into the air.

'You've done splendidly!' Margesson said, beaming, pumping Ogilvie's hand.

'It's not been undiluted success, sir. The guns...'

'What about the guns?' Margesson looked around, frowning.

'I have none, sir. They were taken by the Nawab's men, and the whole battery killed. I'm sorry, sir.'

'You have the Grand Duchess, Ogilvie, and with her back I can forgive the loss of the guns. How is the Grand Duchess?'

'She is well, sir, but it's been a long ride, and there was no food to speak of.'

Margesson nodded understandingly: promising rest and food for all, he announced that he would hear Ogilvie's full report while he ate; Ogilvie first told the Brigadier-General of the vital help of Ayub Shaikh, ex-*Duffardar*-Major of The Guides, indicating that the old soldier had given up his whole future with the Nawab's army in order to render service to the Raj. Margesson promised that the Viceroy would be fully informed and a recommendation made that Ayub Shaikh be found employment within British India. While food and drink was prepared, Ayub Shaikh was closely questioned: his answers were patently honest, but unhelpful. As he had said to Ogilvie, he was a soldier, and had not had the private ear of the Nawab or his political advisers.

The meal was ample, the talk concise and to the point: Margesson listened intently to all the Grand Duchess had to say, nodded without comment when, in speaking of her mission and the treaty, she insisted that she must go forward into Nepal with Count Tomislav. He was visibly moved by the pallor of her face, by the insistent pleading in her eyes. He talked to her, quietly and sympathetically, of London and the court: they had many friends and acquaintances in common, many memories of ceremonial occasions in which they had both played a part when the Princess Elizabeth had been visiting her English relations. They spoke of all this, and the Grand Duchess went on to tell the Brigadier-General something of life in Russia, of the great differences between St Petersburg and Buckingham Palace, of the intrigues, of the difficulties facing her husband the Grand Duke in his Governor-Generalship of Moscow, a city largely hostile to his administration. At the end Margesson said abruptly and with evident reluctance, 'I'm under certain orders, Ma'am. I have to obey them.'

'Orders to give me safe conduct to Nepal, General Margesson.'

'No.' He shook his head. 'I have received fresh orders from my Divisional Commander in Peshawar. I'm to return you there forthwith, Ma'am.'

She stared back at him, her face drained. 'I see. From whom do these fresh orders come, may I ask?'

'You may, Ma'am. From His Excellency the Viceroy.'

'And before that, from my grandmother?'

Margesson looked down at the cloth-covered table. 'The source was not specified, Ma'am – that is, not officially as I understand it.'

'But you believe I am right?'

'I'm sorry, Ma'am. I can say no more than I have said already.'

There were tears in the Grand Duchess's eyes when she said a little unsteadily, 'And you, of course, must do Her Majesty's bidding.'

'And that of the Raj, Ma'am. I serve that interest too.'

'The treaty?'

Margesson inclined his head. 'Yes, Ma'am. It is clearly not in the British interest. You have said as much. I admire your honesty and integrity.'

'Do you, General Margesson?' There was bitterness and sadness in her voice. 'To whom am I loyal, to whom disloyal? The conflict is always here.' She laid a white hand on her breast and stared unseeingly past the Brigadier-General into the far distances, across the Jhelum River and its sluggish, brown-coloured water towards the great peaks that rose snow-streaked to the skies high above far Kashmir, an unbroken line of mountains that led south and east into the kingdom of Nepal.

'It's the very devil!' Margesson said explosively to Lord Dornoch as Ogilvie and his exhausted company slept in the bivouacs. 'The orders are *plain* enough, of course, and I've no option but to obey them. That is – on the surface!'

'And below the surface–'

'Lies Her Majesty, whom may God preserve! She's a wonderful woman, Dornoch, the very best. But she's not always the best judge of a situation, especially out here.'

'Sir?'

Margesson, striding up and down with Dornoch and his Brigade Major, halted suddenly. 'I've been thinking devilish hard ever since those orders came. I know the Court, I know London, I know the Queen personally, and I know Salisbury personally too. I'm damn certain Salisbury didn't want the Grand Duchess withdrawn, and I happen to know His Excellency in Calcutta had certain schemes in mind – revolving chiefly around the potential of the Political Officers attached to the column coming up from Meerut to Dehra Dun. When this business was handed to him on a plate, he found ways of using it to our advantage – you follow, Dornoch?'

'Yes, I do. You're not proposing to ignore the orders, are you, General?'

Margesson laughed. 'You're a forthright

man, Dornoch! Of course there are dangers, but the answer's yes. The Queen is subject to changes of mind – and to tantrums. The Raj isn't governed by tantrums, Dornoch. And in spite of what we tell the Gentlemen Cadets at Sandhurst, it wasn't won by blind obedience to orders! For the record, I propose not so much to ignore the orders as to carry out the intent of the earlier ones.'

'With respect, sir, you'll not impress General Fettleworth or Murree, or Calcutta, with–'

'With devious reasoning?'

Dornoch laughed. 'Your words, sir, not mine. I was going to say, you'll not impress them by acting as a seer, a prober of intent rather than–'

'Seer be damned! Once we're there we'll be able to protect British interests vis-à-vis the treaty.' Margesson lifted his field-glasses and stared across the Jhelum River. For some while he examined the terrain in silence, then brought down the glasses and thrust them back into their leather case. 'We march out at dawn tomorrow, and head for Dehra Dun. When I don't respond to Fettleworth's despatched orders, I'll bet the column from Meerut won't be cancelled. I'll make a further appraisal when I've spoken to the Political Officers. Yes, Dornoch, what is it?'

Dornoch said, 'Just a thought, sir.'

'Out with it, then.'

'Bright eyes, sir!'

Margesson glared. 'What's that?'

'Bright eyes, and a good-looking woman's pleading. Are you sure you haven't too soft a heart, General?' There was a smile twisting Dornoch's lips, but the eyes held seriousness. 'She was most anxious to reach Katmandu, was she not, and never mind the Raj?'

'For her husband's sake. That's only natural – to say nothing of the fact she's Russian now.'

'I was thinking of the Raj, sir.'

'So am I, as well you know. And don't be so bloody impertinent as to accuse me of letting any damn woman sway my decisions! Brigade Major?'

Black snapped to a salute. 'Sir?'

'My compliments to Count Tomislav. He's to consider himself free to wait upon the Grand Duchess, and I'd be obliged if he would attend Brigade at supper.' As Black saluted and moved away, the Brigadier-General nodded at Lord Dornoch in dismissal. Dornoch saluted and turned away, walking towards his regimental lines in considerable disagreement with the orders. Margesson, now that the Grand Duchess was safely back, was a changed man, over-confident to a degree that verged upon sheer stupidity in Dornoch's view. Whatever the Brigadier-General had had to say about the foundation of the British Raj, orders were still orders and the higher the source the more dangerous was the disobedience thereof ... unless, of course, disobedience should be attended by success!

Supper that evening at Brigade was graced not only by Count Tomislav but by the Grand Duchess and Countess Denarov. The Grand Duchess ate in silence, speaking only rarely and looking much preoccupied though clearly relieved that Margesson had changed his mind. The Countess, a devoted lady-in-waiting, sat by her side and antici-pated all her requirements. Tomislav, to Lord Dornoch's intense irritation, behaved with a grand superciliousness throughout the meal, treating the British officers with a cavalierness that verged on contempt, mak-ing politely-veiled references to the iniquity of his arrest and equally politely phrased threats as to what his Czar would have to say to his kinswoman in Windsor Castle; and eating enormously the while. Rage rose in Dornoch when Count Tomislav went on to speak vindictively of the Regimental Sergeant-Major and his former escort, rage that almost choked him.

'It is inexcusable, General, that peasants should be set to guard a Cossack, an aristocrat of Russia.'

Margesson wiped his lips with a napkin. 'I'm sorry, Count Tomislav. I have already–'

'Creatures of the soil, grubby handed and unlettered. The fat man shouts and is uncouth.'

Margesson's face darkened: Dornoch saw, with pleasure, that he could leave honour in the hands of the Brigadier-General. 'The fat man, Count Tomislav?'

'The fat man with the skirt, and bosoms as big as a woman, a peasant of low order,' Tomislav said casually, baring his long yellow teeth and glaring around the table. His voice was loud and he was enjoying the reactions of his audience who were no doubt apprehensive now of the might of the Czar of All The Russias. 'A most unpleasant person!'

'Really?' Margesson enquired. He turned to his mess corporal, standing behind his chair. 'Corporal Gittins, my compliments to the Regimental Sergeant-Major of the 114th Highlanders. I'd be obliged if he'd attend Brigade ... but wait a moment.' He turned to Tomislav. 'You were about to speak, Count Tomislav?'

'You are about to punish this peasant? Perhaps to flog him as in my country would be done with such a man?'

'No.' Margesson said. 'The fact is, Count Tomislav, you are inclined to talk too much. As you've said, Mr Cunningham is a heavy man. I was about to ask him to be good enough to come here and sit on your damned head for the rest of supper, and shut your mouth for you.' He paused. 'Well? Shall I send for him, Count Tomislav?'

Tomislav's mouth closed like a vice, hiding the appalling teeth. He opened it again to say venomously, 'All the British are peasants.' He said no more after that, sitting in a stony silence and eating stale bread and cheese.

'Ogilvie Sahib!' There was no response from the sleeping officer, and Ayub Shaikh spoke again. 'Ogilvie Sahib, wake please, it is I, Ayub Shaikh.'

The words penetrated: Ogilvie reacted

fast, reaching for the revolver beside his head. He sat up. 'What is it?'

'No alarm, Ogilvie Sahib. I ask to speak.'

'Speak away, Ayub Shaikh!'

'Yes, Sahib.' The old soldier's voice was low; he squatted beside Ogilvie, his lips close to the British officer's ear. 'Sahib, there is word that the General Sahib intends to take Her Imperial Highness into Nepal–'

'I hadn't heard. I've been sleeping all the time. Go on, Ayub Shaikh.'

'Also that this is against the new orders from the Lieutenant-General Sahib, commanding in Peshawar.'

'Well?'

'Sahib, I...'

'For heaven's sake, Ayub Shaikh, what is it?'

'Sahib, the memsahib must not cross the border into Nepal. I beseech this!'

Ogilvie sat up. 'You have an urgent sound, Ayub Shaikh. Is there something you know, something you have not yet spoken of?'

'Not know. Ogilvie Sahib. It is not precise. It is a vision.'

'A vision!' Ogilvie laughed hollowly, irritated now. 'Are you not too old a man for visions, Ayub Shaikh, for mere dreams to be significant?' He paused. 'Well, you'd better tell me, I suppose! What was this vision?'

'One that blinded me, Ogilvie Sahib, as if with a great light of truth.' The old man was trembling, his face a deathly white mask behind the whiskers. 'A voice, telling me that the memsahib would be safe only until she reached Nepal, and that in Nepal she is to die.'

'Die, how?'

'By a Russian hand.'

Ogilvie felt a sudden shaft of cold down his back. 'Count Tomislav?'

'I do not know,' Ayub Shaikh answered. 'I know only what I have said, that it will be by a Russian hand.'

'You *know*?'

'It is here,' the old man said, laying a hand across his heart. 'I know the voice spoke truth. I beseech you to tell the Brigadier-General Sahib.'

'You don't imagine the Brigadier-General Sahib will act upon a vision, Ayub Shaikh?'

'Perhaps not, but even so, he must be warned.'

Ogilvie shook his head in wonder: the old soldier went on entreating, clearly convinced in his heart of what he was saying, doing his best to convince the British Sahib that his words should be taken seriously. Upon

266

Ogilvie's promise that he would consider all that had been said Ayub Shaikh turned away at last, moving off in the darkness like a wraith from one of his own visions. Ogilvie lay back in his bivouac, half amused, half angry at having been disturbed. But he found that sleep did not come again: something was nagging too hard at his mind. Visions and dreams were insubstantial, nebulous, to be sure ... but this was India, after all, land of holy men, sadhus and priests, of fakirs whose minds protected them from such wholly physical discomforts as beds of nails and the eating of fire. More importantly, Ogilvie's mind was fastened upon what might be a substance in Ayub Shaikh's vision and he fancied that a report, even if only a sardonic one, could do no harm. When the line of troops began to stir with the dawn Ogilvie got up, washed and shaved and dressed decently, and sought out the Colonel. He met, at first, a cool reception; but his theories as to the possible substance persuaded Lord Dornoch to accompany him personally to Brigade. In his tent, Margesson listened in growing amazement and annoyance.

'Stuff-and-nonsense! Damn my eyes, Ogilvie, this is nursery stuff, not for grown men!'

'Yes, sir. I'm sorry–'

'D'you normally report visions to your superior officers?'

'No, sir–'

'Then why bother *me* with this one?'

'Ayub Shaikh was insistent, sir. And I've thought the matter over. I admit the lack of – of material inherent in a vision sir–'

'Oh, you do, do you?' Margesson looked down his nose. 'I'm glad to hear it!'

'But there's a kind of sense, sir, an integrity of meaning.' Ogilvie hesitated, watching the Brigadier-General's face: it was a study in varying emotions. He plunged on before Margesson could utter again. 'Sir, if the Grand Duchess were indeed to die by a Russian hand, I think we could assume that hand wouldn't be too apparent, too openly guilty.'

'What d'you mean, Ogilvie? You talk in riddles. Be precise, can't you?'

'Yes, sir. What I'm suggesting is this: the death of the Grand Duchess – if that's envisaged – could conceivably be so brought about that it could be made to appear to the world to have been a *British* act. I can't see why else the Russians should want to kill her. If blame were to be cast on us, then the Raj would ... well, incur a good deal of hatred, sir.'

Margesson frowned. '*Russian* hatred? The hatred of the unsuspecting Russian people?'

'Yes, sir. The excuse – ready made for war!'

'By God! It's a theory, I'll say that much – and never mind the visionary aspect! On that basis alone ... you mean the Grand Duchess is safe until the treaty's made, then her death subsequently becomes the excuse for its immediate implementation! War with Russian – and *us* the culprits! Is that it?'

'That's it exactly, sir.'

'I'll be buggered!' Margesson brought out a handkerchief and rubbed his face with it, vigorously. Turning to Lord Dornoch he asked, 'Does all this make sense to you, Colonel?'

'The vision or the theory, sir?'

'Oh damn you–'

'I apologise, sir! The theory – well, yes, taking into account past Russian attitudes and practices, it does. May I ask what you propose doing?' Dornoch paused. 'Harder pressure on Count Tomislav, perhaps?'

'I think not,' Margesson answered heavily. 'We'll keep our own counsel, which gives us the advantage of Tomislav.' He looked along the line of bivouacs as the soldiers turned

269

out to make their ablutions and thin smoke rose from the fires of the field-kitchens. 'There's no change in the orders meanwhile, Colonel, if that's what you're waiting for.'

Dornoch said mildly, 'I'd suggest a reappraisal, I think, sir. The dangers—'

'No,' Margesson said flatly. 'I repeat, no change. It's only a theory – tenable, certainly – but with no basis in known fact. And I'm *not* going to be stampeded by any bloody visionaries! Nor shall I report Ogilvie's thoughts back so that they reach the ears of Bloody Francis, who would undoubtedly turn the situation into one of sheer panic. We've been handed a job. We're going to finish it, once and for all.'

After an early breakfast the troops moved out, fording the Jhelum River whose dirty brown water, debris-filled, reached in some cases to their armpits. They carried their rifles high above their heads as they pushed against the water for the eastern bank, thrusting aside the remains of animal carcasses some of which still had vultures ripping at them as they rode sluggishly down river. The heavy equipment – the stoves and utensils of the field-kitchens, the

Maxims, some of the stores – and the mules were taken across on rafts in the care of many hands. The operation was expeditiously completed and the moment all were safely across the order came down from Brigade for the column to re-form with the Royal Strathspeys in the van. Ogilvie and his depleted B Company were an incongruous sight, marching in their native cavalry uniforms as the pipes and drums led the column out. With around 350 miles yet to go, and the Sutlej and other rivers to be forded, before they made the rendezvous below Dehra Dun, they faced an exhausting march to the south and east with the peaks of the Kashmiri hills on the one hand and the terrible parched territory of the Thar desert to the other. Ogilvie, who had been a party to Margesson's deliberations that early morning, could only hope the Brigadier-General's apparent faith in the continuance of the orders for the column out of Meerut would be vindicated.

Chapter 15

'Punkah-Wallah!'

There was no answer. Lieutenant-General Fettleworth, sweating like a roast pig, flapped his hands in a frenzy and yelled again, this time for his corporal in charge of bearers. The corporal appeared round a screen, red in the face, and slammed to attention.

'Yessir!'

'Damn you, man, I'm suffocating! Where's the damn *punkah-wallah*, hey?'

'I'll find out, sir.'

'You'd better!'

'Yessir–'

'And tan his damn backside till it's raw, Corporal, or I'll have you toe-ing the damn punkah line yourself!'

'Yessir.' The corporal of bearers vanished. His voice could be heard outside, screaming blue murder at lazy natives who had got him into trouble. Bloody Francis, swabbing at

face and neck with a large linen handkerchief, sat down at his desk and lifted
an ornate brass bell, which he rang loudly.
His A.D.C., Captain Simmons, came in and
saluted.

'You rang, sir?'

Fettleworth disregarded the obvious. 'I
want the Chief of Staff. Where is he?'

'I can't say, sir–'

'Find out, then.'

'Yes, sir.'

'Well, *get on with it,* then!'

The A.D.C., as though activated by a hidden spring, turned about. Fettleworth sim-
mered, scowling across the thick rugs laid
on the parquet of his office, urgent thoughts
crowding his mind, not the least of them
being the punishment of the missing *punkah-wallah* ... with relief a few moments
later he saw the punkah blades stir into life,
and the hot air moved, cooling a fraction as
it did so. Shortly after, the Chief of Staff
reported.

'Ah – Lakenham.'

'Good morning, sir.'

'Where the devil have you been?'

'At breakfast, sir.'

'Breakfast, breakfast!' Bloody Francis
waved a hand towards the south and east.

273

'There's men apparently lost out there in some damn wilderness and my staff think of breakfast! Sit down, Lakenham.'

Lakenham sat in a basket-work chair that creaked under his weight. 'Is there something new, sir?'

'Yes, there is. Another personal despatch from Murree. Questions are being asked about the Grand Duchess. Where is she, why have I not reported, what am I doing! The answer is, I'm doing nothing! And *that*, Chief of Staff, was *your* advice!'

'I stand by it, sir.'

Fettleworth stared. 'You do, do you?'

'Yes. But am I to gather it doesn't satisfy Sir Iain?'

'You are. More than Sir Iain. I've said before, we must read between the lines. This can't go on, Lakenham. If only I could see some daylight!'

Lakenham nodded, his own face grave now. 'I still stick by what I said, you know. To send another patrol, another force of any strength, will only lead to more frustration all round. The terrain's too big. We have to trust to Margesson's judgement.'

'He may never have got the message.'

'Yes, I agree that's possible.' Lakenham paused. 'Suppose we assume, now, that he

didn't. In that case, he'll go ahead as ordered, won't he ... and he'll be making the
rendezvous with Dashwood's column out of
Meerut–'

'That's been called off by Murree.'

Lakenham showed surprise and concern.
'Has it indeed? May I suggest you ask
Murree to put it rather firmly *on* again?
If Margesson's marching on with the Grand
Duchess, that's an essential part of the
strategy – especially the presence of the
Political Officers–'

'They'll not be needed now, Lakenham.'

'Because the Grand Duchess isn't to cross
into Nepal. My dear sir, if we act upon our
assumption that General Margesson is
totally unaware of that, then Dashwood's
march is quite vital! It's by his mouth, and
perhaps by his alone, that we can be sure of
acquainting Margesson with the new
orders.' Lakenham was more than worried
now. 'The time has come, sir, to be frank
with Murree: we must confess we're out of
communication with the Grand Duchess.
I'll draft out a despatch, sir.'

It was two days later before a response to
Fettleworth's despatch reached Division,
notwithstanding that it had been sent by

ciphered telegraph with some urgency. The reason for the delay became obvious in the reply itself: much consultation had been called for in the interval. Sir Iain Ogilvie made reference to the Viceroy in Calcutta, to the Commander-in-Chief, to the Secretary of State in London, even to Lord Salisbury himself who, Sir Iain inferred but did not precisely indicate, was tactfully avoiding visits to Windsor Castle. The orders contained in the despatch were brief and to the point: the fullest secrecy was to be maintained and Brigadier-General Margesson was to be diverted back to base from the rendezvous south of Dehra Dun by Brigadier-General Dashwood's column which would now march north from Meerut as originally ordered, with Dashwood himself fully briefed as to the Queen's commands. In the interest of secrecy no further contacts were to be attempted, but the Commander-in-Chief had personally ordered a full alert throughout the Northern Army's area and extended manoeuvres were to take place eastwards from Peshawar and Nowshera with troops from Murree, and Mardan, Rawalpindi, Multan and Lahore joining in. Although this was designated as manoeuvres, all units in the command were to be brought to a war footing under cover of the exercise, which would be conducted by the G.O.C., Sir Iain Ogilvie, in person. Lieutenant-General Fettleworth was held responsible for the immediate readiness of the First Division; and there was a broad and unmistakable hint that, this time, the word immediate was to be construed as meaning, in the army's phrase, at once if not sooner.

Fettleworth's anxiety was now of immense proportions: naturally, he had been well aware all along that this was an affair of state, far beyond the scope of normal military operations; after Sir Iain Ogilvie's ominous despatch Fettleworth felt that the whole weight of Parliament and the Empire had settled upon his back.

The long march was taking its toll: Surgeon-Major Corton and the other regimental doctors had their hands more than full and, although much fortitude was being shown, the commissariat wagons were carrying a heavy load of exhausted men. When they dropped out of the line of march, falling slackly by the side of the dusty track, Count Tomislav laughed in the face of Bosom Cunningham as he went to help them.

'A braggart army,' Tomislav sneered.

'We'll give the lie to that, Count Tomislav, sir, when–'

'I have heard it said that an army marches upon its stomach. This marches upon its back.'

'I would have a care, sir, if I were you.' The R.S.M.'s voice was ominous, but Tomislav laughed again, supercilious and arrogant.

'Such weaklings would not last a yard in the Russian snows. They would die of fright at the very thought of General February, like the armies of Napoleon Bounaparte–' He broke off angrily; he had been talking to the retreating, bristling back of Cunningham. An appalling man, with the typical manners of the peasantry but without the proper subservience. In Russian, sergeant-major or not, he would have been flogged until the skin ripped from the bones and under-meat ... Tomislav's lips curled as he watched the undignified withdrawals to the wagons of the supply train. A ragbag army of amateurs, led by officers who had no decent regard for their own station. Common soldiers had a continual need of the lash and the field-gun wheel and even the bullet if they were to fight well and not get above themselves in the process: in Russia the controlling hand was hard, firm, holding men down from the mutinous acts that would otherwise occur. Count Tomislav laughed yet again, loudly, into the unheeding air: very soon now, the ridiculous British, who acted as if Russian staff work did not exist, as though no preparations had been made in Moscow, were going to get the most appalling shock...

The Brigade marched on with meal-breaks and rests during the day, going into bivouacs at nightfall, marching again with the dawn, into the sun, nearing the high mountain-barrier that closed in the kingdom of Nepal. There was a curious absence of any attack on the column: down in the plains there was not even the distant surveillance to which they had become accustomed. It was as though they marched in a vacuum, all hands being held off them until they entered some final valley of death where the grand assault would come. Cunningham kept the minds of the Royal Strathspeys occupied with more mundane thoughts, moving up and down the line with a sharp eye and a loud voice. Back straight, pace-stick rigid beneath his arm, free arm swinging to his step, head held back, helmet square to the world, he knew very well what the men were thinking as he marched along, boots bashing the rocks as though it were a parade-ground: regimental old bastard, all spit and polish and loud voice, a stickler for tradition and for the proper respects to officers and N.C.O.s and for correctness of dress, the old bugger who knew the precise whereabouts of every bootlace in the battalion and who was always there on their tails like a nanny. But he knew also that, like nanny, he represented security to the men, and a kind of continuance. That was the final grouting-in of his satisfaction in his job.

The days and nights passed, rivers were forded, the advance continued: the careful map-reading at Brigade told Margesson, at last, that they were not far off Dehra Dun.

During the midday halt, he placed the tip of a pencil on the map. 'We're there,' he said to Lord Dornoch. 'And *there*,' he added, indicating a small circular dot, 'is the rendezvous.'

'A day's march.'

Margesson nodded. 'One day to a final decision!'

'No conclusions yet, sir?'

'I'm getting there!' Margesson laughed. 'As a matter of fact, I think I've been there all along. I made the point some while ago that we've been handed the job and have to finish it.'

'You're going through to Nepal?'

Margesson said, 'That must depend on what word we get when we join up with the Meerut column, but currently that's my intention, yes.'

'And if the column doesn't rendezvous?'

'Well, then it really is up to us, isn't it?'

Dornoch said warningly, 'I think you should remember the orders, sir.'

'We've been into that,' Margesson said crisply, and rolled up the map. Dornoch, looking up suddenly, caught the watchful eye of Count Tomislav, staring from a little way off and looking sardonic. Tomislav, mockingly, sketched a salute. Dornoch took no notice of the Russian's action, but was more that ever perturbed by the man's manner ... if it were up to him, he would have placed the Count in arrest again for the security of them all, but had to admit that in all conscience there was not much Tomislav could do on his own. Nevertheless, worry niggled at Dornoch's mind as he took the maps from the Brigadier-General and re-stowed them in their case. Tomislav appeared so confounded confident! And why not, since Margesson seemed to be playing into his hands? Dornoch was preoccupied during luncheon at the Brigadier-General's table, convinced that the life of the Grand Duchess was being jeopardised by Margesson's apparently ready-made decision to continue into Nepal, though he could understand the logic of his reasoning. That afternoon the march was continued, as it had continued so many, many times before. Now they were heading a little to the south of Dehra Dun and straight for the mountains of Nepal. Soon after the rendezvous they would march in the shadow of the foothills of high Himalaya, with a long way yet to go before they turned to the north to head through the passes for Katmandu. Next day, after the night's bivouac, they came down upon the circled spot on the map, between Dehra Dun and Saharanpur. With the foothills lifting to the east, and range upon range of higher peaks, snow-covered, behind the foothills, Margesson brought the column to a halt.

'Fall out and stand easy, Brigade Major,' he said.

'Sir!'

'It's early, but you can sound for luncheon. We may have a long wait.'

'Sir!' Black wheeled his horse and rode down the column. Margesson, still sitting his horse, brought out his field-glasses and with Lord Dornoch stared in silence towards the south. There was a good deal of haze around, but little else, and nothing moving. There was a coolish breeze coming down from the hills and soon, perhaps, the haze over the distant south prospect would clear. Dornoch shivered suddenly: it was not due to the mountain breeze but to a strange feeling of desolation, of being at the world's end. There was a curious silence; the men and animals were moving about as usual, and the field-kitchens were being activated, and Cunningham was lifting his voice against military sin. But in some odd way it was all muted ... some quirk of the atmosphere, or of imagination?

Dornoch asked, 'Do you notice anything, General?'

'Notice what?'

'I don't know.' Dornoch said with a touch of unease in his voice. 'It's something more spiritual than physical, I fancy!' He laughed, but failed to sound amused.

'Spiritual, Colonel? Damn it, man, you've been too long on the Frontier for that!'

'Perhaps that's why.'

'Going soft in the head, my dear fellow? Too much sun?' This time, Margesson laughed. 'Allow me to recommend you for a posting to the winter chills of Whitehall! They're all crazy in the War Office – you'll be in good company. Spiritual!' He snorted. He was about to say something further when Dornoch laid a hand on his arm, peremptorily.

'Listen, sir.'

'I hear nothing! What is it, Dornoch?'

'I don't yet know, sir. A drumming.' He paused, hand held to his ear. 'Distantly, to the south. I believe it's horsemen.'

'The column from Meerut–'

'No sir. That was to be an infantry brigade–'

'But with mounted companies–' Margesson broke off. He said, 'Yes, I hear it now. And ... Good God, Dornoch, look – look there, in the haze!'

Dornoch had seen it already: a mounting thickening cloud of dust, billowing through the sun-haze, climbing above it, extending outwards towards the resting line, accompanied by the growing thunder of horses' hooves and then by the sight of rank upon rank of rifle-brandishing men, a screaming horde of natives in turbans and flowing garments riding down like the wind.

Margesson gasped in horror, and turned in his saddle. 'Bugler!'

'Sir?'

'Sound the alarm! Send the Brigade Major to me instantly! The brigade will form square and fight to the last man in protection of the Grand Duchess.'

Followed by Lord Dornoch, the Brigadier-General spurred his horse and went at a gallop towards the centre of the line. As the notes of the urgent bugles stirred the quiet air, the regiments stood to with their rifles and were herded into formation, like sheep into a pen, by the yelling colour-sergeants and corporals, and were still forming when the native cavalry broke upon them with fire and sword like some devil's contingent out of Hell.

Chapter 16

To the shame of everyone, it was all over within minutes, minutes in which there had been cruel slaughter: the dead and wounded lay everywhere in grotesque, undignified attitudes, and blood stained the dust all around. It had been efficiently carried out and the element of surprise had been well exploited. A group of some twenty riders had cut out the Brigadier-General and brought him down from his horse: he was now in heavy chains behind one of the native cavalrymen. At the same time another group had ridden straight for the Grand Duchess and held her surrounded with rusty bayonets. On the way in through the British line they had slashed and torn and shot. The soldiers, faltering when they saw that both the Brigadier-General and the Grand Duchess had been taken, had been given no chance to rally under the officers. Sweeping down the flanks, the riders had poured in a hail of bullets and then ridden their horses over the wounded to press home the attack in strength. And then, over the sounds of the fighting and the choking screams of dying men, a British bugle had sounded out the Cease Fire and in a voice that shook with emotion the Brigadier-General himself had called the order to lay down arms rather than risk the threatened murder of the Grand Duchess.

Ogilvie, his face grey and streaked with blood, saw Lord Dornoch with a rifle in his back, Cunningham with another, and then saw Count Tomislav, mounted again, now, riding towards the Brigadier-General and smiling in triumph. He heard the Russian's voice, loud with scorn.

'Now the tables are turned, General, it will be you who shall ride – or rather, walk – under escort!'

Margesson's face was grimly controlled. 'This is your work, I take it?'

'None other! You British are such fools. Until I came under your escort this side of the Khyber, I was in excellent touch with Moscow by cable – I had a field telegraph running back to Kabul. The British plans were known, and our General Staff were able to make proper provision–'

'A Russian spy network inside the Raj, Count Tomislav?'

Tomislav laughed. 'Let us say, chiefly inside Afghanistan – but much boastful noise inside the British Raj, a sad lack of secrecy that took little time to reveal your Viceroy's mind to listening ears across the border. In the first place a British escort was necessary, but from this point on the embarrassment of a strong British force was not wanted. We are now near enough to Nepal, provided we enter by a route different from that chosen by your high command–'

'What about the column marching up from Meerut?'

Tomislav, in high good spirits, said, 'They are unavoidably detained, General Margesson, and will not be joining. Their progress was slowed by harassment, and they are now held in a valley by heavy artillery. Do not count upon them, General, I beseech you.'

'And Her Imperial Highness?'

'Goes as planned into Nepal, of course – in *my* charge.' Tomislav turned to the leader of the native cavalry. 'We march when you're ready, Manzoor Khan.'

Margesson asked, 'May I know the route, Count Tomislav?'

'Certainly! There is a pass near Hardwar, a little known pass that leads into the Lesser Himalayas ... whence we enter Nepal on its western border, near Tanakpur.' Tomislav smiled down from his horse. 'A very long walk, General. May God have mercy upon your feet.'

Margesson snapped. 'And may the devil take yours!'

The cruel onward march took its due toll: many of the men were left to die along the track as they moved up into the cold of Himalaya. Margesson, though fighting to the last to keep on his feet, was reduced to a shambles by the weight of his chains and the unaccustomed footwork, to say nothing of the increased pain from his newly-jointed collar-bone. Lord Dornoch, also hurt in the attack, soon joined him in the comparative comfort of the supply wagons, each heavily guarded by armed men. The Colonel of the York and Lancasters, also the officer who had taken over the Border Regiment on the earlier death of his colonel, had both been left behind dead and unburied and now, for some reason, Tomislav seemed to wish to preserve as many of the remaining senior officers as possible – probably, as Cunningham remarked to Ogilvie, for gloating purposes later.

Ogilvie laughed harshly, 'I've no doubt you're right, Sar'nt-Major!'

'I'd as soon die, myself, sir.'

Ogilvie gave a quick sideways look as they plodded on. 'Don't take it too hard, Mr Cunningham.'

The R.S.M. snorted. 'What other way can I take it, Captain Ogilvie, I ask you!'

'If you ask, I'll tell you: hopefully! We still have a potential.'

'Have we, sir?'

'Of course we have! Now look, Sar'nt-Major: if one of the men talked like that, what would you say? Just tell me that!'

Cunningham managed a rather shame-faced smile. 'Why, Captain Ogilvie, I'd certainly not be lost for strong words!'

'That's my Bosom,' Ogilvie said, using Cunningham's regimental nickname. 'As it happens, I have a plan. Or anyway, the makings of one.'

'Sir?'

'It's not so much a plan – yet – as a re-muster.'

'I don't follow, sir.'

'No? Keep your voice down, Sar'nt-Major. We don't know if any of these bandits have some English.' Ogilvie paused. 'Do you like our present company, Sar'nt-Major?'

Cunningham looked puzzled. 'Present company, sir?'

'Look around you.'

Cunningham did so: ahead were a group of privates, some of the Borders, some from the York and Lancasters, one from the Royal Strathspeys. Behind was a lance-corporal from the Border Regiment together with some natives from the supply train. Cunningham said, 'They're all right, sir, but I'd sooner be marching with our own, of course–'

'That's what I meant. With your own unit, you fight better – that's always the case. Now, these natives are not too bright and sometimes don't watch all that closely during the rest periods – I wouldn't risk a break-out, but I believe they'd not notice a little reshuffling of battalions. Now do you understand, Sar'nt-Major?'

Cunningham nodded. 'As you said earlier, a re-muster. Yes, I understand, sir.'

'You'll pass the word, and help?'

'Of course, sir. Aye ... it's a good idea, as a start!'

'As a start,' Ogilvie agreed, smiling. 'Very well, I'll contrive a word with Captain

Black, who's still on his feet.' He paused. 'We'll talk of other things for now, Sar'nt-Major, and I'll come back to you later about the re-muster.'

They walked on between the guards, talking of this and that, of their homes in Scotland and the regimental depot at Invermore, whose wild backdrop of the Monadliath Mountains in Inverness-shire was so similar to much of the Frontier lands. Later in the march Ogilvie slipped up alongside Andrew Black. Black, whose bony face was an almost transparent white, listened in silence while Ogilvie propounded. Black was uneasy, and kept casting glances at the native escort. 'Have a care, James,' he said in a low voice. 'We don't wish to exacerbate the situation by talking liberties.'

'Liberties? My dear Andrew, liberty is what this is all about–'

'I still say, take care!'

'All right. But are you with me?'

'I don't know. This is a very sudden suggestion, James.'

'So was the attack that's made it necessary.'

'Yes, yes.' Black shambled on, his face working with anxiety. 'A word with the Colonel first, I think.'

'Of course. And the Brigadier-General. This has to be co-ordinated.'

'Indeed yes.'

'Will you speak to the Colonel, Andrew?'

Black nodded, somewhat too quickly. 'Yes. Oh yes I will certainly.' He hesitated. 'If you ask me, success is doubtful. These natives are not fools, James, no more is Count Tomislav. They'll smell a rat, and then the shooting will start.'

Ogilvie looked hard at Black. 'Then you'll not be recommending it to the Colonel or to Brigade, Andrew?'

'I shall report your suggestion if and when the chance arises. Any decision will scarcely be mine, will it?' Black winced: his feet were in bad shape. 'Leave it to me, James, just leave it to me.'

Black refused to say more. Ogilvie was under no illusions as to what would be represented to the Colonel and Margesson, if ever Black happened to find the opportunity, which most likely he would see to it that he did not. The Brigadier Major seemed to have lost his spirit, perhaps trusting to some sort of mercy being shown by Count Tomislav if he gave no trouble: it was remarkable, Ogilvie thought, what fear could induce men to pin their hopes on! As soon as it was reasonably possible Ogilvie dropped down the line until he was caught up by the commissariat wagons and found himself close by the Brigadier-General. He saluted the recumbent figure and asked if he was comfortable.

'Comfort is a matter of degree, Captain Ogilvie. I'm more comfortable than the men who're still on their feet.' Margesson's eyes held a shrewd and questioning look. 'What is it you want?'

'A word, sir.'

'Then walk there, by the tail of the wagon. These men have no English – but be brief, Ogilvie.'

'Yes, sir.' In a couple of sentences, Ogilvie conveyed his ideas to the Brigadier-General. 'I've no plans beyond that, but at least we'll be back in formation again.'

'Yes. To be in brigade shape again – a boost for morale, I fancy! You've spoken to your Colonel?'

'No, sir. Only to the Brigade Major.'

'Well?'

Ogilvie hesitated. 'Captain Black ... agreed to represent it to you, sir.'

'Then why have you beaten him to it, Ogilvie?' There was a silence. Margesson broke it, giving a grim but understanding smile. 'All right, my dear fellow, don't answer that. Go and have words with Lord Dornoch, and then with the officers commanding the other battalions.'

'You approve, sir?'

'Yes, I approve. We'll be better placed to take a chance, perhaps. Use the utmost care.'

'Yes, sir.'

'Good luck, Ogilvie.'

Ogilvie saluted, and moved clear of the wagon. He watched the native cavalry guards covertly: he was convinced that no suspicions had been aroused, but the need for circumspection was obvious. For one thing, it must not be he alone who did all the co-ordinating. Neither must all the initial activity be seen to be carried out by the Scots officers: as Black had rightly said, Count Tomislav was no fool. Ogilvie had to accept also that there must be no rushing it: they had time in hand yet, much time before they could reach Katmandu, though on the other side of the picture was the fact that each mile of march took them farther from any likelihood of the Meerut column catching up with them. Ogilvie forced down a natural impatience, and not until that evening did he approach the Colonel in his wagon. Lord Dornoch, in accepting the orders gladly, advised him to use other ranks rather than officers for passing the instructions on, and to be very wary of Count Tomislav. The Royal Strathspeys, he said, should be left till the last. A muster of kilts would be too obvious. 'And another thing, James,' he said.

'Yes, Colonel?'

'Of itself, it's negative. A step in the right direction, but inherently incomplete! There must be *point* in what we do.'

'Colonel—'

'I'll go a stage further for you, James. You'll see to it, when the re-muster has been carried out and all the men fully understand their orders, that we seize Count Tomislav. It can be done, and this is how we shall do it...'

The re-muster was carried out efficiently and free of any untoward incident: all N.C.O.s were quietly contacted by their officers on the march or at rest, and the N.C.O.s moved among the men, dropping words here and there. The orders were welcome enough: already there had been some spontaneous attempt to seek out friends and regimental comrades, and fresh

heart was put into the ranks by the knowledge that the officers were doing something
positive. It became almost a sport: a point
was scored each time a man insinuated
himself into his proper section, marching
once again under his own lance-corporal.
The result could be seen in straighter
shoulders, in faces with more hope in them;
but apparently Count Tomislav, riding
ahead of the native cavalry, noticed nothing
to disturb his self-satisfaction. Now and
again whilst the slow re-muster was in
progress, he rode back down the line, raising
clouds of dust that swept over the men, to
parade his arrogance before Margesson, to
sneer down at the disabled officers in the
rumbling wagons. Cunningham drew Ogilvie's attention to this.

'A good moment to make use of sir, if he
does that again.'

'Take Count Tomislav, and at the same
time safeguard the General?'

'Aye, sir, and the Colonel too, the wagons
being nearly adjacent.'

'I'll bear it in mind,' Ogilvie said. He
looked around at the plodding soldiers: his
Scots were still, in accordance with the
orders, scattered throughout the guarded
column though many had dropped back a

little towards the rear, an almost instinctive movement, it seemed, towards the Colonel. With Lord Dornoch the rallying-point, it would indeed go badly with the Russian if he was caught in the vicinity! A hard, cold knot of anger had settled in Ogilvie's vitals, anger that had mounted steadily since the day of humiliation. He knew this feeling was shared with every man in the brigade and that this time, once Tomislav was in their hands, unarmed as they were, the sneering Russian would not get away alive. And there were better ways of taking him, Ogilvie fancied, than waiting for him to ride down the column at his own chosen moment; thus, that night when the advance into Nepal was halted, Ogilvie made his further dispositions in consultation with the acting battalion commanders.

Ogilvie spoke in Pushtu, addressing the native in charge of the posted sentries: 'I wish words with Count Tomislav. The General Sahib is sick, and may die. Before he dies, he wishes to see Count Tomislav.'

The man peered through the moonlit night, searching Ogilvie's face. 'If the General Sahib, by the will of Mahomet, dies, Count Tomislav will not be pleased.

You have doctors.'

'Yes, we have doctors. If permission is given, they will attend the General Sahib. This will be done quicker if I am allowed words with Count Tomislav. Have a care for your own life, my friend, and do not provoke Mahomet by angering Count Tomislav!'

There was a pause: Ogilvie saw the long-barrelled rifle come up, and felt the pressure of the bayonet as it penetrated his clothing. The man said, 'Come. You shall go. I shall take you. Walk slowly and with care, Captain Sahib.'

Ogilvie turned towards the head of the column, picking his way between the British soldiers and their watchful native guards. The moon's silver light flickered off the regimental badges on tunic-collars and shoulder-straps, off buttons and belt-buckles. There was an eeriness as he walked along, an eeriness that was heightened by a tense silence, a curious emanation of the men's knowledge, passed rapidly by word of mouth not long before, that the moment of action was about to break. Ogilvie felt the gaze of hundreds of pairs of eyes, could almost feel the heavenward passage of the men's heartfelt prayers for a successful outcome. He himself was praying hard as he approached Count Tomislav's well-guarded bivouac behind a jut of rock. His escort called out ahead of his arrival, giving a warning in Pushtu, and Ogilvie saw the Russian's haughty face emerging from thick blankets as the tent-flap was opened. Another man came forward with a lighted storm lantern, and shone it on Ogilvie.

'What's this?' Tomislav demanded.

'The Brigadier-General. He's a sick man and needs medical attention. He wants to speak to you.'

'He does, does he?' Tomislav laughed. 'I am always available for an audience, to those who wish it and have something worth my while to listen to! Let him come to me, Captain Ogilvie.'

'He can't. He's too ill. He asks that you go to him.'

'The wagon can be brought here,' Tomislav said arrogantly. 'I do not go to defeated generals, Captain Ogilvie–'

'Any movement might be fatal. You know the nature of the track without my telling you.' The night was wickedly cold, but Ogilvie's face steamed sweat. 'I don't know what he wants to tell you ... but he sounded urgent.'

'And he sends you, one of his own officers, to fetch me so that I may hear ... something, presumably, that is advantageous to me?'

'I don't know what it is,' Ogilvie said again. 'It may not be advantageous. But you can't doubt that it's important.'

'No?'

Ogilvie shrugged. 'It's your decision, Count Tomislav.'

'Yes.' The lantern threw shadows that moved across the jags of rock as the moon slid away behind a bank of cloud. From somewhere in the distance animal sounds came, savage sounds of hunting and death. The Russian's eyes glittered in the yellow lantern light, and he reached a decision. 'I will come. You will come with me, and think about the rifle in your back.' Tomislav pushed aside his blankets and got to his feet, gesturing to the native guards to remain with him and the British officer. Ahead of the Russian, Ogilvie moved back along the pass. The moon came out from behind the cloud, shining down again, hard and bright and revealing.

Chapter 17

Tomislav had moved towards the commissariat wagon where Margesson lay. The moon shone in through the back, under the canvas cover: its light on Margesson's face made him look truly ill, the flesh white, the eyed darkly shadowed pools. Tomislav said, 'I am here. You may speak, and I shall listen, but quickly. The night is cold, and I am tired.'

Margesson's mouth opened. There seemed to be fresh blood on the sling supporting his left arm. No words came: just a sighing sound. Tomislav moved closer, looking irritated.

'Speak, please! I have no time to waste.'

'A little ... little closer. I am weak.'

It was scarcely above a whisper, just enough for Tomislav to hear it. He bent the upper part of his body, bringing his head down over Margesson's face. An arm came up like a snake, crooked around Tomislav's neck and squeezed hard. There was a gurgle from the Russian, an animal sound deep in his throat. Ogilvie dropped flat, squirmed over, and jerked the native guard off his feet. As the man crashed down, Ogilvie grabbed for the rifle and twisted it away, slamming the heel of his boot into the bearded face. As he did so he yelled out loudly into the night, giving the call for action. After that there was general pandemonium, with men shouting and figures running fast towards Ogilvie. There was rifle fire, but it seemed to lack direction, an indiscriminate loosing-off in a panic reaction. Ogilvie lunged with the bayonet, sliced it through the throat of an attacking native, pulled it out and lunged again. Beside him was the Regimental Sergeant-Major, also with a rifle and breathing heavily as he swung it, using it as a club to smash men's heads. A strong guard of the Royal Strathspeys had closed in around the Colonel's wagon, while men of the Border Regiment had rushed Tomislav, almost strangled by Margesson. Tomislav was now a prisoner in the centre of a half-company, hemmed in and held fast. Several men had seized rifles in the general scrimmage, and were forming a screen, loose enough but so far effective, around the perimeter of the sudden action.

Ogilvie jumped up on the shafts of Mar-gesson's wagon, shouting in Pushtu. Bullets zipped past his head: from the British circle two rifles crashed out, and a native toppled from a spur of rock, his rifle falling with a clatter on to the track.

'We have Count Tomislav!' Ogilvie shout-ed. 'We have him, and if necessary we will put him to death. It is in your hands. Let him tell you himself!' He looked down at the soldiers. 'Sar'nt-Major?'

'Sir?'

'Your bayonet, Sar'nt-Major. Put it at Count Tomislav's throat. When I give the word, kill him. You understand?'

'I understand well, sir,' Cunningham shouted back. 'It'll be a pleasure!' He lifted his rifle and laid the rusted end of the bayonet against Count Tomislav's adam's-apple. 'Now, ye bastard, hold still or in it goes. I can't wait, so don't tempt me!' He paused, then called to Ogilvie. 'All's well, sir!'

Ogilvie nodded. 'Thank you, Sar'nt-Major. Count Tomislav, have you orders for your mercenaries, or have you not?'

There was a hush: the whole arena waited for Tomislav to speak, but no words came.

Tomislav was looking into Cunningham's eyes and seeing no comfort. He licked his lips, the small movement causing his adam's-apple to ride up. The tip of the bayonet grazed and drew a trickle of blood. Tomislav risked more grazing and turned his head towards Ogilvie.

'I have heard it said that the British do not kill in cold blood,' he said hoarsely.

'At the moment, my blood's not cold, Count Tomislav.'

'Nevertheless, I am at your mercy, I admit it. I am defenceless. You will not – I know this – you will not kill a defenceless man.'

Another hush came: Ogilvie sweated. There was truth in what Tomislav had said, but he could not be allowed to win that way, however much it went against training and tradition. It was Cunningham who settled matters. Cunningham, using his parade-ground voice, addressed the Russian. 'Count Tomislav, Captain Ogilvie is not behind the bayonet. I am. Look at me, Count Tomislav. Look at me, I say ... *look into my eyes, man!*'

The hush returned. Tomislav turned his head and looked, and saw his death warrant. Cunningham said, more quietly now, 'You called me a stupid peasant, Count Tomislav.

You called us a braggart army. You said we marched upon our back, that we would die of fright. It'll not be fright alone you die of, Count Tomislav, but dirty steel and a slit gullet. Oh, I'll kill all right, never doubt it! I'm exceeding my orders now, but if you don't do as the officer says you're a dead man. Now – the orders to your natives – if you please! Call them off at once.'

Tomislav said nothing; his mouth was a thin line, tight shut. In the moonlight, hard and brilliant, Ogilvie watched the Russian's face. If the man didn't speak soon, the moment would be lost: the natives would swing into a strong assault. It was touch and go; it was not unlikely that Tomislav, Colonel of Cossacks, preferred to die rather than surrender. Ogilvie saw the shine of sweat on the Regimental Sergeant-Major's leathery face. Cunningham would probably, in fact, not kill a defenceless man, however convincing his tone. Tomislav might decide the gamble was worth while. Many things went quickly through Ogilvie's mind and one thought came uppermost: if Tomislav died, any possible usefulness would die with him. The situation might still turn against the British and the last card would have been played already...

Ogilvie called out sharply. 'Mr Cunningham!'

'Sir?'

'Count Tomislav is not to die yet. We'll not leave matters to him in this way. Keep your bayonet where it is, and the moment there is any attack from the natives – *then* he dies.' Ogilvie turned, lifted his voice clear and strong to the silent, watchful tribesmen, speaking in Pushtu. 'Men of the hills, you have eyes to see what has happened. If you attack, then the Russian dies, leaving you with no support. Consider this well.'

He stopped, staring into an intense silence, waiting for some response, some sign. In that silence he could hear Tomislav's heavy breathing, could sense the man's fear. He saw Cunningham, rock steady behind the bayonet's steel, holding the point firmly against the Russian's throat. They were an isolated group, the centre of an appalling stage of possible slaughter, doomed to certain extinction if the tribesmen on the hillsides should decide to make it so. Ogilvie felt the run of his own sweat, saw the tense look on Margesson's face as the Brigadier-General stared from the back of the commissariat wagon. Not a man spoke: all down the British line they stood and waited as if for a miracle. Ogilvie wondered if he should say more, drive home the lesson of Russian power held at the British bayonet's end. Then Cunningham spoke, in a hoarse but low voice. 'They've taken the point, sir. They see there's no more in it for them!'

At first Ogilvie noticed nothing but a vague blurring of the shadowed figures on the British flanks, accompanied by a curiously formless sound, a kind of rustling, and then, as a movement started in the British lines, a movement of men towards the General's wagon, he realised what was taking place: the natives were fading away in ones and twos, departing over the hillsides and easterly along the track for Himalaya, not as an organised body but as individuals who had chosen discretion and were leaving Count Tomislav to face the music.

Ogilvie breathed deep and let the air go again in a long sigh. 'All right, Sar'nt-Major,' he said. 'Count Tomislav can live, but see he doesn't get away.'

'Well, Dornoch?' Margesson lifted his body on his good arm. 'What's the state?'

'The column's depleted, as you know, sir, but fit to march.' Lord Dornoch looked down upon the men, taking their ease by the side of the track as the sun came up: they were armed once again, the rifles and other equipment having been discovered stowed in the wagons of the commissariat and ammunition train. 'The question is, where shall we march!'

'East and then south, Colonel, taking Tomislav's route as indicated.'

Dornoch stared. 'Into Nepal ... still into Nepal?'

'Still into Nepal – yes.' Margesson's voice was hard. 'Do you question the order, Lord Dornoch?'

'By God I do,' Dornoch answered heatedly. 'Surely, sir, it's obvious enough by now that you're risking the Grand Duchess's life, and in the face of Her Majesty's own order to return her–'

'We're dealing with Russians, Dornoch – with St Petersburg, not Windsor Castle. The Queen's displeasure I'll risk, but I'll not be accused of neglecting my duty–'

'But a woman's life–'

Margesson seemed to brush this aside, brusquely. 'Russian power's at an end for the present purpose. It has to remain that way, Dornoch, for the future security of the Raj. Don't you understand?'

'I do not, sir.'

Margesson said, 'Then I'll explain. For the present, Tomislav's beaten – I agree, as to that. But the Russians are both resilient and patient, and like the phoenix, Dornoch, can rise again. In other words, they'll try again another day – unless they're well and truly shown up as having nothing to offer in Nepal!' He gave a sudden chuckle. 'Have you seen Count Tomislav this morning, Colonel?'

'Yes.'

'How does he look?'

'A sorry sight!'

'Exactly! Not impressive to the Nepalese. Remember there's still a warlike treaty in the balance, Dornoch. It's my duty – *our* duty – to circumvent it.' Margesson was wishing before God that he had been joined by the Political Officers, but there it was, he hadn't and that was that.

'But surely,' Dornoch persisted, 'to take the Grand Duchess on into Nepal is to–'

'I do not propose to over-estimate your Captain Ogilvie's weighty theories, Colonel. In any case, his hypothetical threat is not the only one she faces. She faces others – in Moscow and St Petersburg. It's all very well for the Queen to stand upon her position as a grandmother. The fact remains, it's not up to her – is it? Even she can't abduct a Russian Grand Duchess and expect to get away with it!'

Dornoch laughed. 'Are you suggesting that we should save Her Majesty from the consequences of her own impulsiveness?'

'Indirectly, yes.'

'I quite fail to see how.'

'So do I, but a way will come, Dornoch. The fact is that Queen Victoria or no, if she lives the Grand Duchess must in the end return to her husband in Moscow and her brother-in-law in St Petersburg. I wish her to return in honour and safety. I wish to save her face in her own adopted country. And I consider that to be very much more in line with the Queen's wishes than – than a paltry-minded retreat to the safety of Peshawar with everything left unresolved!'

'The General,' Lord Dornoch said, speaking to James Ogilvie when the march for the Nepal border had been resumed, 'is playing at politics. I'm not given to criticising my superior officer, so I won't do so now. I appreciate the General's arguments fully and as acting Chief of Staff will carry out his orders to the end – though, and this is between you and me, James – I'm damned if I know what the devil he hopes to do in Nepal.' He hesitated. 'Frankly, it's the Grand Duchess I'm worried about.'

'I understand, Colonel.'

Dornoch glanced sideways. 'Well, I hope you do, for I'm damned if I can put it all into words! However, I can be precise about one thing, and it's this: I want a guard upon her and the Countess Denarov. Discreet to the point of being unofficial – but effective, and with you in charge. It's to be operative from now until we're back in cantonments, but with special reference to the time we spend inside Nepal.'

'She's already got an escort, Colonel.'

'I know,' Dornoch said impatiently. 'You'll mount an extra watch – I don't want her out of your sight. I hold you personally responsible for her life, James. You'll detail a half-company with a colour-sergeant and two corporals, the best men you have.'

'Very good, Colonel.'

'I'll have a word with Captain Black.' Again Dornoch hesitated. 'I believe the General intends to make use of the lady in some way – I don't know what. Naturally he intends no harm, but politics is a game a damn sight more dangerous than war some-times, and things can go sadly wrong. Bear it in mind, James.'

Ogilvie saluted and turned away to head down the column in search of Colour-Sergeant Burnett. He was troubled by the Colonel's manner as well as by his words: it was fairly clear that Lord Dornoch was not fully in agreement with the orders of Brigade, and Dornoch knew the dangers of India as well as any man and better than Margesson; and poor old Ayub Shaikh ... but a vision was only a vision, after all! Riding down the line of march, Ogilvie passed by Tomislav and his close escort, and caught the look of blind hate in the Russian's eyes. Tomislav would not forget last night's work, and Ogilvie knew himself to be in personal danger from that direction. Riding on, he found Colour-Sergeant Burnett, and called him out of the column. He passed the Colonel's order, instructing Burnett to bring half his company back to re-form in the rear of the Grand Duchess and her personal guard, and to keep his eyes skinned for trouble.

'It's an unprecedented situation and potentially with the very gravest consequences.'

'Her Majesty—'

'Her Majesty doesn't help by authorising

313

peremptory telegrams!' His face deeply perturbed, Lord Elgin moved along the great Marble Hall of Government House, past the tall white pillars, listening to the dismal racket outside, the sound of teeming rain and tempest: the rains had come at last, long delayed and making up for time lost. The whole vast building seemed to be a-shake; in the night windows had been smashed and the *gilnils* blown in with reverberating cracks like gunfire as the wooden slats split to allow horizontal entry to the wind-driven downpour. Dressing, the Viceroy had disturbed crickets and black beetles; the atmosphere had been that of a hothouse whilst the hurricane had raged outside. The annual move to the Simla hills had been too long put off: Lord Elgin had been unwilling to shift his headquarters in the midst of the worst crisis to occur so far during his tenure of the Viceroyalty, and now he regretted procrastination bitterly. The rain and the howling wind were distracting and somehow ominous, portents rushing ahead of the Queen's displeasure and distress. To lose a member of her family was unthinkable yet had to be thought about; impossible, yet had happened. The extended manoeuvres of the Northern

Army had produced nothing except the terrible tidings that Brigadier-General Dashwood's brigade out of Meerut had been ambushed and delayed for long enough to miss the rendezvous with Margesson. Lord Elgin, filled with gloomy foreboding, paced on. Beside him Sir Iain Ogilvie, hastily summoned from Murree, was urging desperate action, was talking of a possible state of war resulting if the Grand Duchess was not found quickly. It was true that Her Majesty's attitude was to say the least unhelpful to a hard-pressed Viceroy: but it was also a natural one, and one that would undoubtedly find support from her peoples at home and overseas, who had never taken kindly to any tweaking of the lion's tail; and this time it was no tweak; it was a veritable wrench, a haul to the roots from a strong and determined hand...

Sir Iain, clearing his throat, urged on. 'I'm convinced we can't find her by piddling about, Your Excellency. The Queen should never have interfered in the first place, but since she has, the consequences are in our laps. We must act as duty demands, and quickly!'

'What, in precise terms, are you suggesting?'

'That we should cross into Nepal in strength, and take Katmandu.'

'And just what do you suppose that will achieve, General?'

'Frighten the bloody Nepalese, sir! Make 'em see sense before it's too late.'

'Before they sign any treaty or whatever?'

Sir Iain nodded and said robustly, 'We must show the flag, sir. Show the natives the Raj is aware and ready. And–'

'And the Grand Duchess?'

'I'd like a full-scale search along the whole route to Katmandu. At the moment we're hamstrung. Given permission for a full penetration in strength, I'll guarantee to find the Grand Duchess. The moment the Nepalese get the word we're coming in, they'll not dare touch her. This, sir, is a time for boldness.'

'Boldness can lead to war with Russia, if there should be a clash with the Czar's men–'

'That's a risk we must take if necessary.'

'I scarcely think the Prime Minister will be willing, Sir Iain.'

'Then don't tell him!' Sir Iain said energetically. 'Act first, inform after! That has always been my motto, and it has paid off more often than not. You, sir, are Her

Majesty's representative. You are the Raj. Act in its interests – that's my advice!'

Lord Elgin gave a groan and walked on, turning at the end to pace back up the red carpet in the centre of the Marble Hall. Power and splendour, high prestige and obeisances on every hand, his smallest bidding done almost before it had been intimated to his bearers, his *khitmatgars*, even to princes of India – despite all this he was ever at the conflicting mercies of two factions, the politicians and the military. Between them, peer of the realm and Viceroy of India notwithstanding, he felt for all the world like one of the currently-invading cockroaches, to be squashed flat by uncompromising feet. Lord Elgin, pacing in a terrible dilemma, found his thinking overly pervaded by unviceregal reflections upon family relationships and a monumental distaste for granddaughters...

Now the peaks held their quota of watchers: ragged-looking men – small men, different from the Pathans of the North West Frontier – looked down distantly upon the marching column. Himalaya reared mightily, above and ahead, stretching to the everlasting snows at the world's roof. To enter the ancient kingdom of Nepal, lying upon the borders of Tibet, not far below China, was to enter shrouded mystery. A closed land, with queasy overtones of the tomb. They were in fact some way from the border, but already the aura was stealing out insidiously, heralded by the silent watch from the heights. Men thought of *kukris,* the great curved disembowelling knives of the ghurkas. Captain Black came riding down the column towards Ogilvie, and turned to join him.

'Your vigil starts in earnest shortly, James.'

'Yes.'

'Keep your eyes open!'

'I intend to. Why the special adjuration?'

Black smiled. 'Just a thought. A strange land! And as a believer in visions, you are about to enter the danger zone, are you not?'

'I have that well in mind, don't worry.'

'I am much relieved to hear it, James. I have the feeling the Russian is not beaten yet – if he is, then I'm a Dutchman! With your particular responsibilities in mind, you would do well to ponder on that.' Giving Ogilvie no chance to respond, the Adjutant-cum-Brigade Major turned his horse and rode away.

Chapter 18

Black's words had been unnecessary, just one more manifestation of his officious, prod-nose personality: as such they rankled. Their truth was all too obvious. Tomislav could well be, as it were, biding his time – confident yet of some particular outcome in his favour even though he personally was in British custody. What outcome? Something to do with His Highness in distant Bandalpur? It was certain enough the Nawab would have friends, allies, other men of power who might do his bidding when the edict came, either before or after the column crossed into Nepal: the kingdom of Nepal was large enough in all conscience, with much ground to cover to Katmandu. It was desolate, lonely, sparsely populated. An attack, inspired by Bandalpur, could come at any time without the knowledge of the Nepal government, though of course it could be considered possible that an army might be sent from Katmandu as extra backing for the Grand Duchess in Nepalese territory. Tomislav, questioned earlier by Margesson on this and other matters, had refused any information and the Brigadier-General had been unable to shake him out of his arrogant silences. It was scarcely the province of a junior regimental officer to attempt to improve upon his Brigade Commander's performance; yet in view of what Black had referred to as his "particular responsibilities" Ogilvie fancied that a further word might not come amiss. Handing over the personal escort to Colour-Sergeant Burnett, he rode ahead towards Count Tomislav, who was stumbling along between four hard-faced Highland soldiers commanded by a corporal.

Ogilvie reined in his horse. 'Corporal Phillips?'

'Sir?'

'I'd like a word with Count Tomislav. Withdraw the escort, but keep them handy.'

'Sir, I have my orders, and—'

'They're countermanded for the moment, Colonel Phillips. The responsibility is mine, not yours. Fall out the escort.'

'Very good, sir.' Phillips gave the orders, and the men detached to the rear. Ogilvie

320

dismounted and handed his horse to one of the privates. He approached the Russian Colonel, a hand on the butt of the revolver in his holster.

'I shall march with you for a while, Count Tomislav,' he said.

'Why?'

Ogilvie smiled. 'You are a Colonel of Cossacks, an officer and a gentleman—'

'And you are a young fool, to think that flattery will help you. You wish me to speak. I shall not speak.' Tomislav's face was dark, almost devilish with anger and scorn. 'You British are all alike. You blow hot, you blow cold, you bully and you cajole. I have nothing to say to you – to any of you. You are a detestable race.'

'I'm sorry,' Ogilvie said mildly. 'I wished only to be courteous, to speak as one officer to another—'

'And to induce me to indiscretions, which you shall not. I spit on you.' Tomislav followed the words with the action: Ogilvie dodged the stream of saliva, and in dodging stumbled over a piece of rock. He heard the shouted warning from the escort in the rear, but before he could collect himself Tomislav was upon him like a wild cat, clinging to his back and bringing him to the ground with a crash that beat the breath from his body. Firing started, and then, on a shout from the corporal of the escort, abruptly ceased: the target was an unsafe one as the men on the ground fought and struggled for supremacy. At one moment Tomislav was on top, the next Ogilvie: the Russian's hands were around Ogilvie's throat, squeezing hard, nails digging cruelly into flesh. Breathing like a steam engine, Tomislav seemed to have steel sinews. As they fought and rolled in the dust, Tomislav began lifting Ogilvie's head and bringing it down hard against the small rocks scattered along the track, seemingly determined to kill before he was dragged away. As the other men closed in, Ogilvie, seeing nothing now but a red blur, felt Tomislav's grip on his throat loosen and a hand feel for his revolver. Using all his strength he brought a knee up into the Russian's stomach and levered at him with it. No use: Tomislav held fast like a leech, wrenching Ogilvie over so that once more the British officer lay on him like a shield. As Tomislav jerked out the revolver he let go of Ogilvie's throat. An uncertain degree of sight returned: Ogilvie made out a native figure – old Ayub Shaikh, flinging himself bodily onto the Colonel of

Cossacks. And in that split-second, the Russian fired with Ogilvie's revolver, point blank. Ayub Shaikh fell forward with a bullet through his throat. There was a terrible rasping sound and a gush of blood. One of the escort fired without orders, and the revolver spun out of Tomislav's hand. Ogilvie dragged him up, ordering the soldiers to hold their fire: Tomislav had to be preserved – but he did not have to be preserved intact. Ogilvie's fist took him smack on the jaw, and he went down in the dust with his teeth loosened and blood spilling from split lips.

'A stupid action, Ogilvie.' Margesson's voice was cold. 'It could have led to much worse.'

'I'm sorry, sir. I was hasty.' Ogilvie paused. 'I'm sorry about Ayub Shaikh, sir, more sorry than I can say.'

'I don't doubt it, Ogilvie. However, what's done is done. You'll not interfere with Count Tomislav's escort again, d'you hear me?'

'Yes, sir.'

'And as to Ayub Shaikh, he'll be buried here, of course, but his name shall be restored posthumously to the rolls of the Raj, in full honour, as though he were a serving soldier at his death.' Margesson caught the eye of Captain Black. 'A burial party, if you please, Brigade Major, then we resume the march.' His face softened a little as he laid a hand upon Ogilvie's shoulder. 'Don't dwell on it, that's my advice. It's done and that's that, as I've remarked. I'll say no more – your punishment's self-inflicted, I would guess.'

Wordlessly, Ogilvie saluted and turned away, making back towards the Grand Duchess in rear of the battalion, his heart full of sorrow for old Ayub Shaikh. Count Tomislav had simple murder to answer for now, and might well answer for it to British authority rather than to his Czar once the brigade was marched back to Peshawar. When the burial was over, the march was resumed under a blazing sun. Margesson, Ogilvie began to think, was pressing matters too far. There was some insistent worm in the Brigadier-General's mind that was urging him on, giving him no peace. He was pushing tired men beyond their endurance, and was now in some danger of out-marching his supplies, for some days past issued under the strictest ration by the regimental quartermasters. There had been long marches in history, many of them under terrible conditions – Hannibal's crossing of the Alps, Napoleon's retreat from Moscow, and many others less well equipped than this one, but none of them, in Ogilvie's reading of history, had been made in flat dismissal of orders or as escort to so potential a danger to world peace as was the Grand Duchess Sergius. The capacity of Margesson's brigade to fight any pitched battles was growing demonstrably less as the long, cruel days dragged by. Forty-four days from cantonments in Peshawar, something under six hundred miles made good, another four hundred or so yet to be marched and ridden before the column entered Katmandu. God alone could tell what that worm in Margesson's mind might yet lead them into! But, curiously in the circumstances, the Brigadier-General was confident that everything would turn out in the best interest of the Raj and of the Queen-Empress. So the march continued, plodding onward through the mountain passes by day, making their bivouacs in the worsening chill of the night as the height above sea level increased towards the frontier of Nepal, watched still by the little men on the peaks; and Ogilvie and his half-company riding shotgun, as it were, on the Grand Duchess.

Through the pass to the south of Hardwar, the column crossed the border, advancing into seemingly unending mountain vistas and forest-covered hillsides. They were half a day's march inside the border when from some rising ground ahead a heliograph began flashing out a message to Brigade, an urgent signal from the advanced scouts found by the attached patrol of the Duke of Cornwall's Light Infantry. A signaller read off the message, repeating it letter by letter to another man with a note pad, then approached the Brigadier-General. 'Sir! From the scouts, sir—'

'Get on with it, man!'

'Yes, sir. There's an army across the track, estimated to be five thousand men with support artillery—'

'Good God!'

'—but with flags of truce visible, sir. Also an elephant with a howdah. Position, three miles ahead, sir.'

Margesson nodded. 'Tell Mr Barnes-Wilson to halt his scouts and await Brigade. Well, Dornoch, what do we make of this? Friend or foe?'

'The flag of truce, sir—'

'Doesn't mean a thing – damn it, Dornoch, you're supposed to know India!'

'I do, and I disagree. Nepal's a friendly country – so far! They'll not dishonour a flag of truce, sir.'

'How do we know they're Nepalese, for God's sake?'

'We must take that on trust, sir.'

'They could be Bandalpur's bandits!'

'I doubt it, sir. They'll scarcely have had the time to outflank us.'

'But we can't be sure!'

'No sir, we can't. But we've come a devil of a long way at great cost and we're right out on our own. We mustn't risk a mistake now, sir. There's far too much in the balance.'

Margesson fidgeted, rasping a hand over his moustache. 'Are you suggesting we also march under a flag of truce?'

'I am, sir. As you said – I know India. There's no disgrace in the white flat out here!'

The Brigadier-General gave a ghost of a smile. 'Your diplomatic side coming out, Dornoch!'

'That's how it has to be, sir.'

'Very well, we'll advance peacefully till we're given cause to do otherwise. Brigade Major?'

Black rode his horse forward and saluted. 'Sir?'

'Kindly inform the battalion commanders of the situation. There will be no hostile acts unless I pass the word by bugle for action. But the men will be fully alert and will march smartly, not as a rabble thinking of surrender – nothing like that.'

'Very good, sir–'

'My aim will be to impress and give the buggers food for thought if they have notions of a surprise attack. We march with the drums beating, and the pipes and fifes. That's all, Brigade Major. Now where's my A.D.C.?'

'Sir?'

'A bedsheet, Captain Parsons. One of my own. Hoist it on a rifle and carry it ahead of the Brigade.'

'Sir!'

'Before you do that, I want words with Count Tomislav. Have him brought before me, if you please.' Margesson, with the column standing easy behind him, waited impatiently. Within the next two minutes Count Tomislav was marched up by a colour-sergeant and escort of four privates, and halted by the General's horse. 'Now, Count Tomislav,' Margesson said, staring down at the Russian, 'you'll perhaps have heard we're confronted by an army which may be Nepalese. Have you any comment to offer?'

Tomislav laughed in his face. 'What comment do you wish, General?'

'I wish to know if you were expecting such an army, had things gone according to your plan.'

'I do not know. I cannot read minds. I am no prophet.'

'You will have been given orders, the orders usually include advices.'

'Mine,' Tomislav said insolently, 'did not.'

Margesson nodded, his mouth tight. 'Very well, Count Tomislav. You will march ahead of my horse, where I can keep a personal eye upon you.' He turned again to Lord Dornoch. 'The Grand Duchess, Colonel. She's to be preserved at all costs. If fighting should start, she's to be taken to the rear with a strong escort, you understand?'

'I understand, sir.'

'Good. Sound the advance, if you please.'

The buglers blew and the battalion commanders marched their men out to the beat of the drummers, with the colour-sergeants shouting the step. Soon, as they approached the rise in the track and Brigade, breasting it, came within the view of the army below, word was passed for the wind instruments. Ahead of Brigade, the pipes of the 114th Highlanders began wailing out along the pass, immediately smartening the column. Ogilvie, as his close-escort company came with the Grand Duchess to the crest of the rise, looked down upon a splendid and colourful scene, one that took the breath away: rank upon rank of men in a long column that wound back along the pass, snaking away between the tree-clad slopes of the hills, all with rifles and bayonets and wearing dark uniforms; beside them down the column were the mule-borne guns of mountain artillery for all the world like British batteries. These guns has not been assembled for action: Ogilvie guessed there would be much relief at Brigade. Ahead of the main column but behind a well-armed vanguard of infantry was a brilliant splash of colour provided by a personal escort, mounted on white horses and with guidons fluttering from lances, around a massive elephant carrying a canopied howdah with rich drapings that caught the afternoon sun in rainbow colours of blue and red, purple and gold and green. The British column moved on behind the pipes and drums until the two flags of truce were within a dozen yards of each other; then the bugles sounded again and the pipes died away.

Margesson, standing in his stirrups and gazing towards an old man seated in the howdah, called: 'I come in peace, representing Her Imperial Majesty Queen Victoria, and her Viceroy in Calcutta. Do you meet me in peace?'

There was an almost ghostly silence in the pass: nothing seemed to move, nor a man even to breathe. It was a claustrophobic moment and an extended one: Margesson, his nerves on edge, was virtually on the brink of sounding for action so as to get the first blow in when the old man spoke from the back of the elephant, his voice high and uncertain with age. 'You are met in peace, General Sahib. We are good friends of the great British Raj.'

Margesson moistened his lips. 'Long may it remain so,' he called back. 'To whom have I the boundless honour of speaking?'

The reply came from the splendidly-clad native in command of the personal escort: 'You speak to His Highness Maharaja Bikram Bahadur Kali Pratrap Rana.'

'Do I by God!' Margesson muttered at Dornoch. 'Who the devil's he when he's at home – d'you know?'

'Rana, sir. The Rana family ... hereditary Prime Ministers since 1846.'

Margesson stared. 'The Prime Minister himself? He ranks above the king, doesn't he?'

'He carries more weight, shall we say.'

Margesson cleared his throat and lifted his voice again. 'I am much honoured by Your Highness. I present the good wishes and intentions of the Queen-Empress.' He glowered for moment, uncertain of what he should say next. 'May you live a thousand years,' he called down along the silence of the pass.

The ancient figure bowed his head. 'May Her Imperial Majesty the Queen-Empress live also a thousand years.'

Margesson sucked in breath and muttered again at Lord Dornoch. 'Should I have included his own monarch, d'you think?'

'It's perhaps advisable, sir.'

'What's his name, then?'

'His Majesty Maharajadhiraja–'

'Oh, that'll do.' Margesson called once more. 'May His Majesty the King of Nepal also live for a thousand years.' He gave a cough: Count Tomislav was turning round and grinning up at him. Enough time, Margesson felt, had been spent on the greeting. 'Your Highness, have you come to give me escort to Katmandu? Is this your intention?'

There was another silence, broken this time by the faint sighing of a wind that had started blowing along the pass, a cold wind. Then the old Prime Minister said, 'That is not my intention, General Sahib. I come to talk. Tidings have come to Katmandu.'

'What tidings, Your Highness?'

'Tidings of the activities of the Nawab of Bandalpur. I come because the journey to Katmandu holds possible dangers for the high personage in your charge General Sahib. We shall talk here ... the high personage, the representative of the Czar of All The Russias, and myself. No-one else. I–'

'And I, Your Highness? Am not I to be a party to the discussions, as representing the Queen-Empress?'

'Many regrets, General Sahib. You are but the escort. I now ask you to accompany us to a village nearby, where the important matters will be talked about.'

Margesson's face had reddened: to his staff the situation looked dangers. Lord Dornoch laid a hand on the Brigadier-General's bridle. 'Take care, sir! You were never invited anyway, remember.'

'D'you mean to say I've simply handed the Grand Duchess over to–'

'Softly, sir, softly. You've done what you came to do. You insisted upon delivering the Grand Duchess in accordance with the original orders. You've done that – not in Katmandu, it's true, but the idea's the same. We've arrived. Now the diplomacy begins – don't you see?'

'See what?'

Dornoch sighed. 'Play this with very great care, sir. Go along with His Highness, but exploit the fact that Tomislav is on his own with his Cossacks beaten. I don't believe His Highness is yet in possession of all the facts.'

'But the Grand Duchess – she may go and conclude something, bring off this confounded treaty!'

'No doubt she'll attempt to. She must be headed off, but with honour to herself, and safety when she returns to Russia.' Dornoch paused. 'It's a tall order, I know, but I've told you before, sir, out here a soldier's always fifty per cent diplomat. Bring this off and you'll end Russian aspirations for the next fifty years!'

His face like thunder, Brigadier-General

Margesson gave the order to advance. With the pipes and drums, and the fifes, all silent the British column moved between the equally silent ranks of the native infantry, past the guns, with the escorted elephant and its rich howdah trampling along ahead of Brigade. The Nepalese began the march alongside them, still in peace but with the rifles ready in their hands and a look of watchfulness in their faces. Margesson's thunderous expression was very largely due to the insistence of His Highness the Prime Minister that the Russian officer be produced. Margesson had had no alternative: Count Tomislav had been produced and freed of his escort, and his first ungracious act had been to put his fingers to his nose and waggle them towards the Brigadier-General. He had then been invited to approach the howdah, and the elephant's mahout had with cries and proddings of a short stick brought the great grey animal to its knees ... and now Count Tomislav was riding in state, in the howdah with His Highness; and would no doubt be taking the fullest advantage of his position to tell all manner of lies about the British.

Chapter 19

The entered the village, which was no more than a collection of huts in a valley below the pass to the southward. A handful of male inhabitants watched; there were no women in sight as the British regiments marched in with the Nepalese solders on their flanks.

The elephant stopped outside a long, low building, around which a strong guard was at once placed by the Nepalese. As the elephant was brought again to a kneeling position for its howdah passengers to get down, the Brigadier-General rode his horse towards it. 'A word, if you please Your Highness,' he said.

'Speak, General Sahib.'

'I am here, as you said yourself, to act as escort for Her Imperial Highness the Grand Duchess Sergius. To that extent she is my responsibility, and one I cannot abrogate–'

The Grand Duchess,' Count Tomislav

broke in, 'is a Russian charge now, not a British one. *I* can escort her, Your Highness.'

Margesson scowled. 'Your Highness, in Count Tomislav you see all that is left of the Russian Cossack guard. All the rest were slaughtered by the Nawab of Bandalpur. There is no Russian power here in Nepal. Count Tomislav is an empty vessel.'

As Tomislav appeared about to utter harsh words, the old native silenced him with a lifted hand, then smiled at each of the two men in turn. In a soft voice he said, 'Argument is not necessary. Her Imperial Highness will be well guarded by our own soldiers.' He paused. 'There is no desire for Her Imperial Highness to come to harm. She comes as a friend. She is received as a friend with whom we hope and expect to conduct affairs of state. Be assured we shall care well for her.'

Margesson said, 'Your Highness, I fear she may be in some danger.'

'From what source, General Sahib?'

'From the Russians. From Count Tomislav.'

Tomislav said hotly, 'This is nonsense! I am charged by the Czar himself with her safety. If I lose her, I am likely to lose my life. I have, you see, a very personal interest!'

He glared at Margesson.

'And you, General Sahib?'

'I think,; Margesson answered stiffly, 'you are aware of the relationship to Her Majesty Queen Victoria, Your Highness.'

'And if harm came, you would also lose your life?'

'That's unlikely,' Margesson said. 'Nevertheless, I must insist that I be allowed to place a guard of British soldiers on the Grand Duchess whilst the discussions take place, and I further insist that I myself be present in order to represent Her Majesty the Queen-Empress in matters affecting the security of the Raj. Your Highness, I am convinced your own king would grant no less, since he is friendly to the Raj and since there is long-standing agreement between himself and our government in Calcutta. For many years past there has been loyalty in Nepal to the British Raj. This you know well, Your Highness.'

'This I know.' Once again the wizened old face crinkled into a smile and the head bobbed. 'General Sahib, I wish words with Her Imperial Highness the Grand Duchess.'

Margesson hesitated. He caught the eye of Lord Dornoch, who gave an almost imperceptible nod. Margesson said, 'Of course,

Your Highness. Colonel, if you would be so good?'

'Sir!' Dornoch saluted formally. 'Due ceremonial, I take it?'

'What?'

'An important occasion, sir.'

'Oh, very well, very well.'

Again Dornoch saluted, his hand quivering before his Wolseley helmet. He turned and rode down the line. Another curious silence had fallen, broken only by the hoofbeats of the Colonel's horse on the hard ground. The atmosphere was tense, every man watchful. The hillsides closed them in, wrapped them in a small tight world, a meeting place of two Empires, incongruous in its simplicity considering all that was now in the balance. All eyes seemed to be on Dornoch as he rode. He halted beside the Grand Duchess's escort, saluting again.

'The Brigadier-General's compliments, Ma'am. He wishes you to join His Highness Maharaja Bikram Bahadur Kali Pratrap Rana ... Prime Minister of Nepal.' He hesitated, scanning the pale face. 'You're willing, Ma'am?'

'Yes, Lord Dornoch. That is why I came, is it not?'

Dornoch nodded. 'Remember we're here,

Ma'am. We'll not leave you. No escort will be allowed inside the council chamber, but we'll not be far. Captain Ogilvie?'

'Colonel?'

'Your particular orders are suspended for the time being, but you'll provide a captain's escort to Brigade for Her Imperial Highness.'

'Yes, Colonel.'

'Mr Cunningham will accompany you, also the pipes and drums. Do you understand, Captain Ogilvie?'

'I think I do, Colonel. An impressive turnout?'

'Exactly. His Highness is to be reminded of the Raj on his doorstep. Carry on, if you please.'

Ogilvie saluted, and the salute was returned punctiliously by Lord Dornoch, who then turned and rode slowly back towards Brigade, again in a chill silence. Ogilvie sent a messenger for the pipes and drums and for the Regimental Sergeant-Major: Cunningham was quick to report.

'Sir?'

Ogilvie passed the orders: there was an understanding gleam in the R.S.M.'s eye. He about-turned with a parade-ground crash and began bellowing, shattering the silence hanging over the village and the two columns. 'Numbers One and Two sections of B Company will form a dismounted captain's escort to Her Imperial Highness the Grand Duchess Sergius of Russia, the pipe and drums of the battalion leading. Half-company ... atten – *shun!*' As the pipes and drummers marched down from the head of the column to a single drum-beat, the Regimental Sergeant-Major loudly deployed the Highlanders to right and left of the Grand Duchess on her horse, and then reported to Ogilvie.

'Escort ready to advance, Sir!'

'Carry on, if you please, Sar'nt-Major.'

'Sir!' Cunningham turned about. 'Escort ... slope *arms!*' There was a smartly concerted rattle from the rifles. 'Escort, by the right...quick – *march!*' In rear of the soldiers, Cunningham stepped off, pace-stick beneath his arm, loud voice bellowing the step. 'Left ... left ... left, right, left. *Swing those arms.* Keep your heads up!'

The pipes swelled into "The Heroes of Vittoria" and, with the beat of the drums, echoed savagely off the enfolding hills. Ogilvie, riding behind the Grand Duchess, who was accompanied by her lady-in-waiting, and in front of the rearguard of the escort, felt a mounting tension among the men of the British regiments lining the way to Brigade. As he rode along, he looked down at them. Hollow-cheeked, weary men in uniforms caked with the mud from dust and sweat, many of them wearing bandages, blood-stained and dirty – they were still British, and they were being brought to an awareness of it now. The faces were watchful, the eyes narrowed as though the need might soon come for a sudden lifting of rifles, a lunge with the bayonets into native hides. It was a tricky moment: the men of Nepal were not enemies, or at any rate not yet. The results of any loss of temper before the situation clarified could be disastrous, could shake the Raj badly. Ogilvie appreciated the Colonel's desire to use every means of impressing His Highness; but had a fear that the very notes of their pipes might impress the Highlanders more than the Nepalese and cause some hot-headed rashness if the situation should begin to look against them.

At Brigade Margesson waited with Lord Dornoch and Andrew Black. Opposite, across a trodden strip of no-man's-land, waited His Highness together with Count Tomislav. Tomislav was behaving arrogantly and with confidence: his Czar had paved the way for him, and stood metaphorically behind him, together with all the might of Russia. The Grand Duchess would do what was demanded of her by her brother-in-law and he, Count Tomislav, would return in due course to St Petersburg with a treaty of great value in his pocket. This the British could not prevent...

As the pipes and drums of the Royal Strathspeys beat nearer, His Highness cupped a listening hand to an ear grown less acute with age. A curious look came to the monkey-like face: he stared for a moment down the line of men towards the splash of colour provided by the Highland kilts. Then he turned to the Russian.

'You come alone, Count Tomislav Sahib. Why is this?'

Tomislav shrugged. 'The fortunes of war, Your Highness.'

'The British general spoke of slaughter,' His Highness said in a faraway, sing-song voice.

'*I* told you also. My Cossacks were savagely attacked.'

'And beaten?'

Tomislav snapped. 'Russians, Cossacks especially, are never beaten, Your Highness!'

'But are killed?'

'Are killed, yes. When they are killed, they die as soldiers, as men.'

'Yet *you* have reached Nepal.'

'True.' Count Tomislav, about to say a great deal, for he had not liked His Highness's tone, instead shut his mouth with a snap, savagely. A better time would come, and for now the devilish squeal from the men in skirts was drowning all other sound, and the attention of His Highness had in any case wandered. The sound was immense as the Grand Duchess came alongside Brigade, a shatter of noise that assailed Count Tomislav's ears horribly, and then all at once was overborne by the hideous and well-remembered tones of peasantry.

'Escort will halt! Escort ... *halt!*'

The noise stopped. 'Stand *still* there!'

Tomislav very nearly obeyed: memory was still too recent. He scowled, his face dark with self-annoyance. He watched while the British captain, taking over from his terrible peasant, made a flowery report to his general. Then the British general saluted the Grand Duchess, murmured a few words that Tomislav failed to catch, and rode with her across the empty space towards the Nepalese Prime Minister who bowed and scraped with due ceremony.

'Your Imperial Highness is most welcome to our country. You will wish now to rest.'

'Your Highness is kind.' From a little to the right of the Grand Duchess, Lord Dornoch noted that she was paler than ever, and that her hands shook on the reins. There was strain in her voice too; she was beginning to falter at the last. Dornoch glanced sideways at Margesson, saw his look of anxiety and indecision. The Grand Duchess, recovering herself a little, went on, 'A little rest, perhaps, then I shall be ready.'

'I wait upon Your Imperial Highness. You have come. There is much time.' The old man bowed again. 'Our land is at the disposal of Your Imperial Highness, representative of the Czar of All The Russias whom may the gods protect and love.'

'No, not I,' the Grand Duchess said in a low voice. 'Not I, but Count Tomislav, shall conduct business in Nepal.' Very suddenly she burst into tears, covering her face with her hands and letting the reins fall. A sharp look came into the face of His Highness, and Margesson urged his horse forward, placing it firmly between the Grand Duchess and the furious figure of Count Tomislav.

345

'Calm yourself, Count Tomislav!' he said, and turned to the Grand Duchess. 'Ma'am, forgive me, I–' He broke off, swinging his horse to face westerly along the pass. A crack had come, a single shot, its location marked by a white puff of smoke on the hillside. Everyone looked: the hills had come alive with men, infantry and cavalry, and bullets were singing down upon the village. Margesson stood in his stirrups and shouted for his bugler. 'Brigade will deploy and find cover! Prime Minister, you're under attack as well and I advise you to fight with us! Lord Dornoch?'

'Here, sir.' Dornoch was bringing his horse up on its haunches as he turned for his regiment.

'The Grand–' Margesson broke off, staring, searching. 'Where's that feller Tomislav?'

Dornoch looked, Ogilvie looked: there was no sign of the Russian. Dornoch said, 'He's made off, sir. Never fear – he'll be found!'

'He'd better be! See to the Grand Duchess, Colonel. I'm no believer in visions, but if St Petersburg does intend some dirty work in her direction, then now's their chance. And in any event that bugger's not to get away, d'you hear?'

'He won't!' Dornoch called to Ogilvie. 'Captain Ogilvie, resume close escort. Keep out of the fight – that's an order. Your job's the Grand Duchess. Stick to it – and to her.' He swung away as Ogilvie rode up to the side of the Grand Duchess and took her bridle. With the escort of Highlanders around them, they forced their way through the ranks of the Nepalese soldiers, making as fast as possible for the temporary cover of the long building behind, putting its walls between themselves and the attacking army. All around there was the greatest confusion, with the ranks of the British and native armies intermingled, but soon a more or less concerted fire was being directed against the enemy force. There was still no sign of Count Tomislav. Once in the lee of the long hut, Ogilvie tried to reassure the Grand Duchess, but she had broken down and seemed not to hear, and Ogilvie left her to her lady-in-waiting, Countess Denarov; though she was sobbing as brokenly as her mistress, she might give some of the comfort that Ogilvie had not the time for. With Colour-Sergeant Burnett he ran to the corner of the native hut and looked round carefully, dodging back as a bullet almost singed his eyebrows. Burnett said, 'I think we should get out, sir.'

'And I think you're right, Colour Burnett!' Ogilvie looked around, trying to assess the likely chances in the hills: the fighting was concentrated to the south and west, the way to the north seemed clear enough, and Ogilvie decided to withdraw his escort from the village and lie up in the northern hills. He passed the word to Burnett and with the two women in the centre – dismounted so as to present the smallest possible target for the enemy rifles, but with the horses being led – the escort of Highlanders doubled out from behind the hut, dodging and twisting between the other village buildings, making with all speed into the jagged, rock-strewn hills and the trees that grew like a friendly blanket up their steep sides.

'Your Excellency, a word if I may?'

'Come in, Durand. What is it?'

The Military Secretary advanced upon the Viceroy, who was standing with his back to a blazing fire in the drawing room of the private apartments. 'A despatch from the Resident of Katmandu, sir.' He paused: the news was not good. 'I fear there's trouble.'

'Well?'

'The Resident's relying on the bush telegraph admittedly, but he reports a British
column having crossed into Nepal–'

'Margesson's?'

'Not specific, sir. But it's now known in
Katmandu that the Prime Minister's left for
a village, a little place called Parbatti, not far
inside the border. I believe there's a clear
inference to be read.'

Lord Elgin's face lost colour. 'The Grand
Duchess, d'you suppose? A meeting?'

Colonel Durand nodded. 'It's likely
enough, sir – likely enough. If so...' He
didn't finish the sentence: the Viceroy
needed no crossing of t's. The Queen wishes
stood most grossly flouted now. 'Shall I send
for Sir George, sir?

'Do that,' Elgin said harshly. 'Bring maps,
and you may warn Sir George in advance
that I shall want an army corps to advance
into Nepal with the utmost despatch. Infantry – cavalry – field-gun batteries. He
must telegraph at once to Sir Iain Ogilvie,
who should by now have reached Meerut by
the train – Northern Command has strong
forces handy for Nepal. I can only pray
they'll get there in time.' He paced the
room, moving towards one of the great windows, staring unseeingly into the teeming

wet of the monsoon. 'In the meantime, Colonel, we must prepare a telegram for London, and break our silence.'

Chapter 20

They made away from the village, moving at the double with the Grand Duchess held like a sack of potatoes on the broad back of a private, her arms around his neck and his hands supporting her thighs. Another soldier carried the Countess Denarov. When they were far enough and in good cover Ogilvie called a halt. He looked down through the trees at the fighting, with Burnett by his side.

'The bastards,' Burnett said, breathing heavily with the exertions of the uphill dash. 'The Nawab of Bandalpur, no doubt!'

Ogilvie nodded: 'Likely enough, though I don't see his uniforms.'

'He'll no' be wanting to advertise, sir!'

Ogilvie went on looking through his field-glasses: the fighting was confused in the extreme, with small groups engaged everywhere, and bloody fighting it was. Lord Dornoch was galloping down the line with

351

Andrew Black behind him, both men slashing with their claymores. The Brigadier-General was nowhere to be seen, but as Ogilvie watched a bugle blew and the men of the York and Lancaster Regiment went forward at the charge behind gleaming bayonets, rushing for a strong body of native infantry drawn to one side of the track. As the bayonet charge scattered the native force, Margesson was seen, dismounted and staggering about, his sling freshly blood-stained and his face cut by a sword. As the fighting milled around, an officer of the York and Lancasters slid down from his horse and ran towards the Brigadier-General; after this Ogilvie lost sight of them. He was about to speak when Burnett put a hand on his arm and whispered urgently in his ear.

'Someone up here, sir, in the trees. I heard the crack of a branch.'

'You're sure it wasn't one of ours?'

'Dead sure, sir. This was away to the right. There's someone stealing up on us, sir.'

Ogilvie kept his glasses trained on the fighting below and gave his orders without moving his head. 'All of you stay where you are. Keep the Grand Duchess close to the ground, and cover her fully. Colour Burnett, remain and take charge.'

352

'What are you going to do, sir?'

'Slip round behind and outflank our visitor.'

'You'll need help, Captain Ogilvie, sir.'

'No. I'll make less commotion on my own. Guard the Grand Duchess, Colour Burnett.'

'With my life, sir.' Burnett's voice was grim. 'And the best o' luck, sir, wi' yon bugger!'

Ogilvie snapped his field-glasses back into their case and dropped flat to the ground, crawling away on his stomach through the undergrowth lying thick between the trees. Apart from his own movement and the distant crack of rifles and the cries of men he could hear nothing, no disturbance of branches close by. Whoever was there was keeping very still: he would be bound to hear Ogilvie's progress. Ogilvie stopped, and lifted his head cautiously. He saw no-one. Very slowly he crawled on, skin of hands and face scratched and bleeding, knees lacerated by rocks lying hidden in the scrubby growth. Moving round behind his Scots, he came up on their right, and stopped again, listening, watching for any movement that would give away a hidden enemy. Nothing happened: time passed, time that might be vital. Margesson's intention had been, clearly, that he should attempt to get the Grand Duchess back across the border and link up with the British forces that must surely by this time have been ordered out on an extended search towards Nepal. They were no more than half a day's march inside the border: the hopes were good if there was sufficient speed, and meanwhile Margesson was occupying the foray from Bandalpur...

Ogilvie sweated. Burnett would easily have been mistaken. He waited a while longer in burning impatience, and was about to rejoin his company when suddenly he saw the faint movement, ahead and a little to his left: there was a high rock, half obscured by the trees, and there was a slowly growing hump coming around its edge, the hump of a man's body, a shoulder, swelling into a torso. Then the outline of a rifle: Ogilvie, his revolver in his hand, leapt to his feet and ran, firing towards the rifle barrel, jumping over the clinging undergrowth. He saw the furious face of Count Tomislav emerge, and then he tripped and went flat on his face. He was aware of a shout from Burnett, and of rifle-fire close by, then he saw Tomislav coming for him regardless of the Scots' fire, with murder in his eyes and his rifle aimed for a killing. Ogilvie twisted sideways, and as he did so squeezed the trigger of his revolver. He missed: so did Tomislav. The Russian sheered off to the left with bullets from Burnett's party zipping like bees around his head. Running nimbly, dodging, leaping over the fronds and scrub like a deer, he vanished, with the Scots in pursuit.

Ogilvie scrambled to his feet. 'Break off!' he yelled. 'Colour Burnett – the Grand Duchess!' He ran back towards the Grand Duchess, who was still on the ground but sitting up. 'Are you all right, Ma'am?'

She smiled. 'Oh yes, I am all right, Captain Ogilvie. Was that Count Tomislav?'

'It was Ma'am.' Ogilvie turned to the escort as they came running back. 'Leave him, Colour Burnett, it's pointless to walk into his range. We'll keep together, and keep a careful watch. When we come into more open ground ... then he'll have to show himself.'

'Aye, sir.' Burnett tweaked at his moustache. 'And the orders now, sir?'

'We head west for the border and we don't stop till we cross it–'

'And leave the regiment, Captain Ogilvie?'

Ogilvie said, 'Those are the orders, Colour-Sar'nt. We have the whole load now –

and the regiment's giving us a clear field out.'

Burnett grinned, a savage grimace. 'You hope, Captain, sir – you hope! And so do I.'

They marched or rode in silence, concentrating all their energies on the main chance. Dead tired, and unwashed, they struggled through the terrible mountains towards the border, keeping their eyes skinned for evidence of the solitary pursuing Russian. There was water in the water-bottles and each man carried the iron rations issued at the start of the march against just such an emergency: hard weevily biscuits and concentrated chocolate tablets. Nothing else: and they would need to watch carefully the expenditure of ammunition. Breaking the silence Burnett ventured to suggest a criticism of the Brigadier-General. 'We'd have done better not to go in at all, sir.'

'Not necessarily, Colour Burnett.'

'How so, sir? We've not achieved much!' His laugh was sardonic, bitter.

'We can't say that yet. Time'll give the right answer. A British promise has been kept, at least. And I've a strong feeling a treaty's been abrogated before it was even made!'

Burnett sighed, shading his eyes along the terrible track. 'Aye ... you might be right, sir. I suppose it could be said yon Nawab back there did us a bit o' good without meaning to! Though he'll have made the men pay a heavy price today.'

'That's India, Colour-Sar'nt.'

'Aye, and I'm not sure I've not had too great a bellyful of it, Captain Ogilvie, sir.' Burnett eased his rifle on his shoulder and stared up at the peaks, jagged against the sky's hard outline, watching closely as a corporal sent up the relief for the pickets. They plodded on; the sun was going down now. Not much longer and the twilight would come, and then the cloak of the night. The men and horses needed rest, but to halt and bivouac would be dangerous in the extreme. Ogilvie was balancing the need for speed against the need for rest, when suddenly Burnett spoke sharply. 'Sir, watch the crest – to the right and a little ahead!'

'What is it?' Ogilvie brought up his field-glasses.

'A movement, sir.'

'The pickets–'

'The picket has passed it by, sir, but I

believe–' Burnett broke off. Something had started to move on a wide, flat ridge below one of the crests of the hillside. There was a cracking sound and small rocks flew in the air, and then Ogilvie and Burnett saw the huge irregular chunk falling, bouncing off the hillside in a plunge down into the pass.

Ogilvie roared, 'Scatter – up the hillside to the left, fast as you can!' Just for an instant he saw a tall figure on the heights, silhouetted against the skyline. Then, as Burnett brought up his rifle and took a sight, Ogilvie dashed ahead towards the Grand Duchess, dismounted and grabbed her without ceremony, pulling her from her horse and dragging her towards the left, away from the crashing, spinning boulder. He heard Burnett pumping bullets upwards and then with an appalling judder of the very ground the boulder hit, bounced, and fell again a few yards farther on. There was a scream that seemed to rip the air in two, then the great lump of rock bounded up the lower slope on the far side of the pass, leaping up above the heads of Ogilvie and the Grand Duchess. Just in time before it rolled back in a shower of small rocks and debris, Ogilvie wrenched the Grand Duchess clear and rolled her bodily, over and over to safety.

With horror in his eyes, he looked down into the pass, at a spread of blood around the crushed and broken body of the Countess Denarov. He got to his feet and ran blindly for the farther slope, his revolver firing uselessly up at the heights towards Count Tomislav; then became aware of Burnett shouting at him.

'It's all right, sir! I got the bastard, sir. Look out of his bloody way, now!'

Ogilvie halted. Dashing the sweat and dust from his eyes, he stared upward. Tomislav seemed to claw the very air, his face twisted and devilish, then he toppled. It seemed to Ogilvie after that to happen in slow motion. Twisting, turning, falling and bounding in fearful arcs from the rocky hillside, Tomislav descended to his death, a bloody lump of quivering meat that hit the pass to lie spitted like a pig on a sharp, upstanding sliver of sunset-reddened rock. A curious light-headed feeling came to Ogilvie, a feeling that somewhere in the heights of heaven old Ayub Shaikh was looking down with happiness and sorrow mixed that his vision had pointed the finger of fate at the wrong person.

They bivouacked; now there seemed no

reason to drive weary bones into complete exhaustion. Rested, they moved on westerly with the dawn. After two hours of march, they heard, by this time not unexpectedly, the uplifting but distant sound of the fifes and drums coming down on them from ahead, from towards the border lands. Soon, coming round a bend in the pass from where they could look down into lower-lying regions, they witnessed the massive advance of British power, the prongs of Northern Command's war machine personified by the British and Indian regiments of the line and the proudly waved guidons of The Guides and the Bengal Lancers, and behind the splendour of the cavalry the dull grey of the field-gun batteries moving through the clouds of dust brought up by the limber wheels.

A cheer went up from the small band of Scots, helmets were thrown into the air. Ogilvie looked towards the Grand Duchess: she was weeping freely and openly, but her eyes were shining through the tears: there was clearly a conflict of emotions. As the forces, the great one and the small, converged Ogilvie saw the panoply of high command in the van immediately behind the fifes and drums: and somewhat to his surprise recognised his father. With more than a trace of embarrassment he halted his half-company and went forward.

Sir Iain Ogilvie lifted a hand and the Northern Army came to a halt. The fifes and drums died. Ogilvie saluted and reported formally.

'Captain Ogilvie, 114th Highlanders, sir–'

'Yes, James, we'll take it as read.' Sir Iain, unusually informal, looked away beyond his son. 'How's Her Imperial Highness, h'm?'

'She is well, sir.'

'And just as well you brought her out, my boy!' The General Officer Commanding, trewed and claymored as a Royal Strathspey, rode his horse forward and saluted. 'You're a most welcome sight, Ma'am. I shall have fine tidings for your grandmother.' He turned in his saddle. 'Chief of Staff!'

'Sir?'

'You will kindly have the escort relieved. Fall them out to the wagons. See they're well fed and issue rum. They've earned it, by God!' The General was beaming with pride in his former regiment. 'We'll not delay now. James, your full report at once, and no holding back.'

★ ★ ★

361

In obedience to the orders from Calcutta, Northern Command moved on easterly to make contact with Margesson's column, with drums beating and colours flying out over the dreary waste of the land. Ogilvie, who had asked and been granted permission to accompany the force, rode with his father. The Grand Duchess had been left behind with a commissariat wagon at her disposal and a guard of no less than two infantry battalions, two squadrons of Bengal Lancers, and a field battery, to wait for the G.O.C.'s return. James Ogilvie believed she had come through with honour, that she could return to both England and Russia without fear. She had played her part and let neither country down: even the Czar of All The Russias could scarcely blame her for the attack by the wily Nawab of Bandalpur and if there should be any sour faces in St Petersburg then a rap over the knuckles from Windsor Castle would no longer be inappropriate! Meanwhile in the general advance back into Nepal all units were ready for action and spirits were high. Sir Iain unbent to James to the extent of being gently critical of Brigadier-General Margesson.

'Foolish,' he said. 'Foolish and high-handed, though it sounds as though some good has come of it. A touch of Nelson – it doesn't come amiss at times, but don't take it as an example!'

'No, sir.'

'He could have lost his command.'

'But in fact will not, sir?'

Sir Iain gave a harsh laugh. 'I've said enough to a captain, and propose to say no more. What's that?' The Chief of Staff was riding up, and from ahead a heliograph was winking. 'What's the message, Forrestier?'

'Margesson's brigade is marching in, sir, behind the pipes and drums–'

'Is it, by jove! What shape are they in?'

'Apparently not too bad, sir. They have company: a native force.'

'A *native* force?' Sir Iain glanced at James. 'Bandalpur, no doubt, but I'm damned if I understand it!' Sir Iain lifted his hand to halt the column, and they waited, the tension mounting. Soon the head of the column came into view: Ogilvie saw Lord Dornoch riding in with Margesson; and then he saw Andrew Black with a bandaged head, and Cunningham limping but still clasping his inevitable pace-stick ... a lump came to his throat as the wail and beat of the battalion's pipes and drums sounded loudly and proudly out. Behind the Royal Strath-speys came the elephant-borne howdah with His Highness and another native figure, and behind the elephant a horde of Nepalese and other levies.

The heads of the columns met; salutes were exchanged punctiliously. 'I'm glad to see you,' Sir Iain said, sweeping his glance over the battalions in rear of Margesson. 'I take it the situation's now under control?'

'It is, sir. May I take it you have the Grand Duchess safe?'

'You may indeed.'

'Then I believe the matter is satisfactorily settled, sir. There will be no treaty. The Prime Minister of Nepal is ... appreciative of the power of the Raj.'

'Good! You shall make your detailed report during the march back to Meerut, where your battalion will be properly rested before returning to Peshawar.' Sir Iain raised a hand and indicated the richly-caparisoned elephant and the two occu-pants of the howdah. 'Is one of those Bandalpur?'

'Yes,' Margesson said, looking angry.

'A captive?'

'Not exactly, sir. He wishes words with you.'

'Then he shall have them! He's supposed to be a friendly b– prince.' Sir Iain looked shrewdly at the Brigadier-General. 'Have you words for my private ear, General?'

Margesson blew out his cheeks. 'I have, yes. Plenty! The Nawab considers himself to have been instrumental in saving the life of the Grand Duchess – and in settling the hash of Count Tomislav – and in finishing off the treaty that–'

'I thought he had attacked your column, Brigadier-General Margesson?'

'So did I, sir – and he did! He insists that it was all a mistake. He was under the impression we were Russians! He attacked in the interest of the Grand Duchess, and of the Raj.'

'And now he expects his just reward – is that it?'

'As I gather, sir – yes.'

Sir Iain looked down the column between the peaks past the Royal Strathspeys. The elephant's hangings were a splash of brilliant colour beneath the sun: in the howdah the two occupants sat gravely nodding and grinning, the one like an ancient nut, the other bloated, greasy and horrible. Sir Iain gave an involuntary sigh: India was, as ever, India. Margesson, late of the Brigade of

Guards, would scarcely understand; but he must not be allowed to upset the even tenor of diplomacy. Face was everything, and Bandalpur was a useful ally. Loathsome but useful – and Lord Elgin wanted no storms in any case. As for Whitehall, Lord Salisbury was himself a diplomat by training; and the Queen could consider she had got her way. Matters could have been a great deal worse – a great deal! Sir Iain turned towards Margesson again. 'So be it,' he said. 'I know he's a bloody liar, but Her Majesty will not be found stingy.' Margesson's face was a picture as the G.O.C. rode his horse towards the column. In Sir Iain's view, it served him right for raising the temperatures of everyone from the Queen down!